Collins
COBUILD

Key Words for
Accounting

HarperCollins Publishers
Westerhill Road
Bishopbriggs
Glasgow
G64 2QT

First Edition 2013

Reprint 10 9 8 7 6 5 4 3 2 1 0

© HarperCollins Publishers 2013

ISBN 978-0-00-748982-4

Collins® and COBUILD® are
registered trademarks of
HarperCollins Publishers Limited

www.collinslanguage.com

A catalogue record for this book is
available from the British Library

CD recorded by Networks SRL,
Milan, Italy

Typeset by Davidson Publishing
Solutions, Glasgow

Printed in Great Britain by Clays Ltd,
St Ives plc

Acknowledgements

We would like to thank those authors
and publishers who kindly gave
permission for copyright material
to be used in the Collins Corpus.
We would also like to thank Times
Newspapers Ltd for providing
valuable data.

Contents

Contributors

Specialist consultant
Mariette Knoblauch, Chartered Professional Accountant,
Ballard Beancounters, Seattle USA

Project manager
Patrick White

Editors
Katherine Carroll
Kate Mohideen
Enid Pearsons
Elizabeth Walter
Kate Woodford

Computing support
Mark Taylor

For the publisher
Gerry Breslin
Lucy Cooper
Kerry Ferguson
Gavin Gray
Elaine Higgleton
Persephone Lock
Ruth O'Donovan
Rosie Pearce
Lisa Sutherland

Introduction

Collins COBUILD Key Words for Accounting is a brand-new vocabulary book for students who want to master the English of Accounting in order to study or work in the field. This title contains the 500 most important English words and phrases relating to Accounting, as well as a range of additional features which have been specially designed to help you to *really* understand and use the language of this specific area.

The main body of the book contains alphabetically organized dictionary-style entries for the key words and phrases of Accounting. These vocabulary items have been specially chosen to fully prepare you for the type of language that you will need in this field. Many are specialized terms that are very specific to this profession and area of study. Others are more common or general words and phrases that are often used in the context of Accounting.

Each word and phrase is explained clearly and precisely, in English that is easy to understand. In addition, each entry is illustrated with examples taken from the Collins Corpus. Of course, you will also find grammatical information about the way that the words and phrases behave.

In amongst the alphabetically organized entries, you will find valuable word-building features that will help you gain a better understanding of this area of English. For example, some features provide extra help with tricky pronunciations, while others pull together groups of related words that can usefully be learned as a set.

At the start of this book you will see lists of words and phrases, helpfully organized by topic area. You can use these lists to revise sets of vocabulary and to prepare for writing tasks. You will also find with this book an MP3 CD, containing a recording of each headword in the book, followed by an example sentence. This will help you to learn and remember pronunciations of words and phrases. Furthermore, the exercise section at the end of this book gives you an opportunity to memorize important words and phrases, to assess what you have learned, and to work out which areas still need attention.

So whether you are studying Accounting, or you are already working in the field and intend to improve your career prospects, we are confident that Collins COBUILD Key Words for Accounting will equip you for success in the future.

Guide to Dictionary Entries

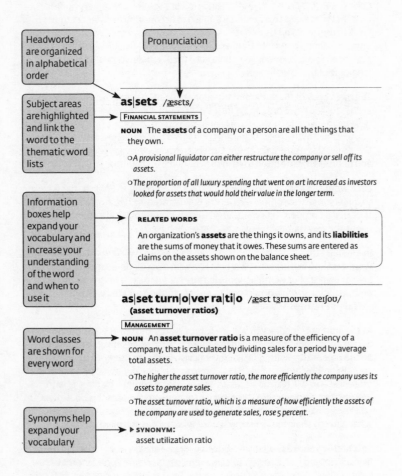

Headwords are organized in alphabetical order

Pronunciation

Subject areas are highlighted and link the word to the thematic word lists

as|sets /ǽsɛts/

FINANCIAL STATEMENTS

NOUN The **assets** of a company or a person are all the things that they own.

○ *A provisional liquidator can either restructure the company or sell off its assets.*

○ *The proportion of all luxury spending that went on art increased as investors looked for assets that would hold their value in the longer term.*

Information boxes help expand your vocabulary and increase your understanding of the word and when to use it

RELATED WORDS

An organization's **assets** are the things it owns, and its **liabilities** are the sums of money that it owes. These sums are entered as claims on the assets shown on the balance sheet.

as|set turn|o|ver ra|ti|o /ǽsɛt tɜ́rnoʊvər reɪʃoʊ/
(asset turnover ratios)

MANAGEMENT

Word classes are shown for every word

NOUN An **asset turnover ratio** is a measure of the efficiency of a company, that is calculated by dividing sales for a period by average total assets.

○ *The higher the asset turnover ratio, the more efficiently the company uses its assets to generate sales.*

○ *The asset turnover ratio, which is a measure of how efficiently the assets of the company are used to generate sales, rose 5 percent.*

Synonyms help expand your vocabulary

▶ SYNONYM:
asset utilization ratio

Guide to Dictionary Entries

Variants of the headword, such as abbreviated, full forms and British forms, are also shown

E|BIT|DA /ɪbɪtdɑ/ (short for **earnings before interest, tax, depreciation and amortization**)

FINANCIAL STATEMENTS: INCOME STATEMENT

ABBREVIATION EBITDA is the amount of profit that a person or company receives before interest, taxes, depreciation, and amortization have been deducted.

Definitions explain what the word means in simple language

○ Supporters of EBITDA as a measure argue that it is a good approximation for operating cash flow because it adds back depreciation and amortization, which are often major non-cash items.

○ The company has managed in three years to boost sales by nearly 400 percent while dramatically increasing both EBITDA and owners' compensation.

Examples show how the word is used in context

mark down /mɑrk daʊn/ (marks down, marked down, marking down)

COMMERCE

All the different forms of the word are listed

VERB If you **mark down** something that you are selling, you reduce the selling price.

○ Rather than marking down menu prices, the chain would offer coupons giving patrons a discount on certain items.

○ If a product is not selling, its price is marked down within a specified period.

▶ COLLOCATIONS:
mark down a price
mark down a product

Collocations help you put the word into practice

Guide to Pronunciation Symbols

Vowel Sounds

ɑ	calm, ah
ɑr	heart, far
æ	act, mass
ɑɪ	dive, cry
ɑɪər	fire, tire
ɑʊ	out, down
ɑʊər	flour, sour
ɛ	met, lend, pen
eɪ	say, weight
ɛər	fair, care
ɪ	fit, win
i	feed, me
ɪər	near, beard
ɒ	lot, spot
oʊ	note, coat
ɔ	claw, bought
ɔr	more, cord
ɔɪ	boy, joint
ʊ	could, stood
u	you, use
ʊər	lure, endure
ɜr	turn, third
ʌ	fund, must
ə	*the first vowel in* about
ər	*the first vowel in* forgotten
i	*the second vowel in* very
u	*the second vowel in* actual

Consonant Sounds

b	bed, rub
d	done, red
f	fit, if
g	good, dog
h	hat, horse
y	yellow, you
k	king, pick
l	lip, bill
ᵊl	handle, panel
m	mat, ram
n	not, tin
ᵊn	hidden, written
p	pay, lip
r	run, read
s	soon, bus
t	talk, bet
v	van, love
w	win, wool
ʍ	why, wheat
z	zoo, buzz
ʃ	ship, wish
ʒ	measure, leisure
ŋ	sing, working
tʃ	cheap, witch
θ	thin, myth
ð	then, other
dʒ	joy, bridge

Word Lists

BASIC

accounting
adjust
adjusting journal entry
advance
agree
allocate
amortization
amount
APR
bank
bankruptcy
billable
bonus
bookkeeping
books
bring forward
bring over
budget
budget for
calendar year
carry forward
carry over
cash
C corporation
check
clear
close out
compensation
control
corporate
corporation
cover
CPA
cumulative
current
customer
default
deficit
double entry
earnings
entity
e.o.m.
extraordinary
fair market value
financial year
fiscal year
funds
gains
general partnership
gross

gross up
hard copy
income
independent contractor
insolvent
insurance
intellectual property
interest
interest rate
license
licensed
limited partnership
liquid assets
liquidity
LLC
loan
long-term
losses
manufacturing
material
modification
net
outstanding
partnership
personal property
petty cash
present value of future cash flows
price
proceeds
product
profit
profitability
pro rata
provision
rate of return
real estate
real property
recognize
recurring
report
reporting
reserve
residual
restricted
retroactive
revenue
salary
sales
S corporation
secured
services

short-term
single entry
subcontract
sublease
subsidiary
surplus
T account
tangible
transaction
translation
transpose
unallocated
unappropriated
unrestricted
valuation
value
wages
year end
yield

COMMERCE
account
advance payment
agreement
bad debt
bank account
bank reconciliation
bank statement
bill
bill of lading
bill of sale
C & F
cash discount
charge
chargeback
check
checking account
check register
check stub
CIF
COD
collect
commission
consignment
contract
credit
credit memo
creditor
debit
debt
debtor

deposit
deposit slip
due date
EFT
expense account
expenses
FOB destination
FOB shipping point
freight-in
freight-out
goods
installment sales
invoice
item
lease
lease-back
lease with option to buy
lessee
lessor
letter of credit
list price
lockbox
margin
mark down
mark-up
merchandise
merchant account
merchant fees
merchant service
negotiable
offer
on account
order
packing slip
past due
payee
payment in advance
payor
postdate
prepayment
purchase order
quote
raw materials
receipt
receipts
receivables
receiver
reconcile an account
refund
reimburse
remit

remittance advice
retail
sales slip
shipment
shipping documents
statement
supplier
terms of payment
trade discount
vendor
void
voucher
warehouse
warehouse receipt
wholesale
wire transfer
withdraw

FINANCIAL STATEMENTS
account
accrual
accrual basis
accrue
annual report
assets
audit
auditor
audit trail
balance
balance an account
book
book depreciation
book-to-tax reconciliation
book value
capital expense
capital gain
capitalize
capital lease
cash basis
cash flow
chart of accounts
classify
close the books
contra account
control
control account
cost of goods available for sale
credit
credit side
current cost
current expenses

debit
debit side
deferral
deferred
entry
financial statements
foot
footing
footnotes
functional currency
GAAP
general journal
general ledger
historical cost
hybrid basis
impairment
intangible assets
item
journal
journal entry
keep the books
ledger
loss on sale
loss on translation
lower of cost or market
mark-to-market
net
net realizable value
normal balance
overstated
post
PPE
pro forma
purchase ledger
reclassify
register
sales ledger
set off
statement of cash flows
statement of earnings and
    comprehensive income
suspense account
trial balance
unbalanced
understated
write down
write-up

Balance sheet
accounts payable
accounts receivable

allowance for bad debts
asset account
balance sheet
balance sheet account
balance sheet equation
capital account
charge
current assets
current liabilities
equity
equity account
fixed assets
goodwill
liabilities
liability account
long-term liabilities
net assets
net asset value
note payable
off
paid-in capital
permanent account
prepaid expense
retained earnings
shareholders' equity
unearned income
write off

Income statement

above the line
administrative expenses
below the line
cash book
cost of goods sold
depreciation expense
EBIT
EBITDA
expense
expense account
gain on sale
gain on translation
gross
gross profit
income account
income statement
loss
net earnings
net income
net loss
net profit
net sales

operating expenses
operating income
other expenses
other income
profit and loss statement
realized gains
realized losses
selling expenses
temporary account
unrealized gains
unrealized losses

INVESTING

bond
capital
capitalization
capitalize
capital stock
collateral
common stock
compound interest
current ratio
debt-to-equity ratio
discounted cash flow
diversification
dividends
dollar cost averaging
earnings per share
face value
gross profit margin
hedge
initial public offering
investment
leverage
margin
market
option
preferred stock
price earnings ratio
principal
promissory note
public company
quick ratio
return
return of capital
return on assets
return on capital
return on equity
return on investment
savings account
securities

share
shareholder
stock
unsecured

MANAGEMENT
allocation
asset turnover ratio
balanced scorecard
beginning inventory
board of directors
break even
breakeven point
budget
carrying charge
cost
cost accounting
cost center
cost overrun
direct
ending inventory
FIFO
finished goods
fixed charge
fixed costs
free cash flow
indirect
internal rate of return
inventory
inventory turnover
LIFO
net present value
operating budget
operating cost
operating margin
operating profit
opportunity cost
overhead
period costs
plant
prime cost
product costs
production
profit center
profit margin

receivables collection period
receivables turnover
revenue stream
standard cost
stock
sunk cost
supply chain
transfer pricing
turnover
value added
variable costs
variance
weighted average cost of capital
working capital
work-in-progress

TAX
capital gain
capital loss
carry back
carry forward
deduction
depreciable
depreciation
expense
income tax
ordinary gain
ordinary loss
straight-line depreciation
tax
taxable
taxation
tax avoidance
tax deductible
tax deduction
tax-deferred
tax depreciation
tax evasion
tax exempt
tax loss
tax rate
tax refund
tax relief
tax return
tax year

A–Z

a|bove the line /əbʌv ðə laɪn/

FINANCIAL STATEMENTS: INCOME STATEMENT

ADJECTIVE **Above the line** income or expenses are entries that appear above a horizontal line on a company's profit and loss account, and show how the profit or loss was made.

○ *Each period, cumulative cash flow is reflected either below the line for cash investments or above the line for returns.*

○ *Losses or negative returns below the line must get subtracted from future profits or gains above the line to calculate the net present value of the company to investors.*

---

ac|count¹ (ABBR **a/c**) /əkaʊnt/ (**accounts**)

FINANCIAL STATEMENTS

NOUN An **account** is a detailed record of all the money that a business or a person receives and spends.

○ *In double entry bookkeeping, every debit or credit in the account is also represented as a credit or debit somewhere else.*

○ *Unless we make an adjustment to lower the original cost figure shown in the accounts, we will be overstating the value of the asset.*

---

ac|count² (ABBR **a/c**) /əkaʊnt/ (**accounts**)

COMMERCE

NOUN An **account** is a record kept by a business of invoices and payments for a customer.

○ *The check for $8000 was an immediate payment on account of the agreed price for the house.*

○ *We have gained some new clients to offset the old clients, but we've probably lost more accounts than we've gained.*

ac|count|ing /əkaʊntɪŋ/

BASIC

NOUN **Accounting** is the activity of keeping financial records.

○ *The purpose of accounting is to provide records of all financial transactions, so that the financial position of a business can be determined.*

○ *Under regulatory accounting practices, that debt can be counted as capital.*

ac|counts pay|a|ble (ABBR **AP**) /əkaʊnts peɪəbᵊl/

FINANCIAL STATEMENTS: BALANCE SHEET

NOUN A company's **accounts payable** are all the money that it owes to other companies for goods or services that it has received, or a list of these companies and the amounts owed to them.

○ *On the liabilities side, the accounts payable to suppliers, wages payable to employees, and taxes payable are current liabilities.*

○ *The company increased its accounts payable, in effect borrowing an additional $7 million from its suppliers.*

ac|counts re|ceiv|a|ble (ABBR **AR**) /əkaʊnts rɪsiːvəbᵊl/

FINANCIAL STATEMENTS: BALANCE SHEET

NOUN A company's **accounts receivable** are all the money that it is owed by other companies for goods or services that it has supplied, or a list of these companies and the amounts that they owe.

○ *When one company sells goods to another company, it does not usually expect to be paid immediately. These unpaid bills, or trade credit, make up the bulk of accounts receivable.*

○ *Most business-to-business transactions involve sales on credit, usually 30-day terms, and that leads to accounts receivable.*

ac|cru|al /əkruːəl/ (accruals)

FINANCIAL STATEMENTS

NOUN An **accrual** is an amount of money that is owed in one accounting period and that has not been paid by the end of it.

○ *We have large accruals for payroll and benefit-related costs.*

○ *Liabilities, including accruals of taxes and other expense items, are deducted from total assets.*

ac|cru|al ba|sis /əkruəl beɪsɪs/

FINANCIAL STATEMENTS

NOUN An **accrual basis** is a system of accounting where income is recognized before payment is received and expenses are recognized before they are paid.

○ *Dividend and interest income is reported on the accrual basis.*

○ *Under the accrual basis, companies record transactions that change a company's financial statements in the periods in which the events occur.*

ac|crue /əkru/ (accrues, accrued, accruing)

FINANCIAL STATEMENTS

VERB If you **accrue** an expense or income, you recognize it before it has been paid or been received.

○ *I owed $5000, part of which was accrued interest.*

○ *An accrued liability is recognized at the end of the period in cases in which an expense has been incurred but cash has not yet been received.*

▶ **COLLOCATIONS:**
accrue expenses
accrue income
accrue interest

ad|just /ədʒʌst/ (adjusts, adjusted, adjusting)

BASIC

VERB If you **adjust** the amount of a transaction or account, you change it.

○ *The insurer automatically adjusts the amount of insurance each year to keep up with rising construction costs in your area.*

○ *The total output of goods and services, adjusted for inflation, rose at a 1.7 percent annual rate.*

ad|just|ing jour|nal en|try (ABBR **AJE**) /ədʒʌstɪŋ dʒɜrnəl ɛntri/ (adjusting journal entries)

BASIC

NOUN An **adjusting journal entry** is a journal entry that is made to correct an error or update an account.

A

○ *Every adjusting journal entry will affect at least one revenue or one expense account.*

○ *The proper method of accounting for bad debts requires an end-of-period adjusting journal entry that reduces both net income and the balance sheet carrying value of accounts receivable.*

---

ad|min|is|tra|tive ex|pens|es /ædmɪnɪstreɪtɪv ɪkspɛnsɪz/

FINANCIAL STATEMENTS: INCOME STATEMENT

NOUN Administrative expenses are business expenses that are not related to the cost of goods or sales, such as salaries of office staff, insurance, and legal and accounting costs.

○ *The company's administrative expenses can be divided into personnel, travel, building occupancy and other similar costs.*

○ *In most straight personal bankruptcy cases there are no assets left after payment of administrative expenses.*

---

ad|vance /ædvæns/ (advances, advanced, advancing)

BASIC

VERB If you **advance** money for promised goods or services, you pay the money before the goods or services are provided.

○ *A syndicate advanced the money to pay for the construction.*

○ *The subcontractor's severe cost overruns made it necessary for the company to advance cash to ensure completion of the project.*

---

ad|vance pay|ment /ædvæns peɪmənt/

COMMERCE

NOUN An **advance payment** is a payment that is made before goods or services are provided.

○ *The company used the money to make an advance payment to the project's owner against future delivery of the product.*

○ *The advance payment is the good-faith money your client pays when you both sign a contract or letter of agreement.*

a|gree¹ /əgri̱/ (agrees, agreed, agreeing)

BASIC

VERB If one number or figure **agrees with** another, or two numbers or figures **agree**, they are consistent with each other.

○ You must ensure that your figures agree with the bank's figures.

○ The totals of the two columns must agree.

a|gree² /əgri̱/ (agrees, agreed, agreeing)

BASIC

VERB If you **agree** one number or figure **with** another, you make them consistent with each other.

○ The Finance Division tried to agree the numbers, so that both sides started from the same base calculations.

○ At the end of each day, you must agree the total recorded with the cash collected.

▸ COLLOCATION:
agree the numbers

a|gree|ment /əgri̱mənt/ (agreements)

COMMERCE

NOUN An **agreement** is a plan or a decision that two or more people have made.

○ Under the agreement, all domestic accounts would be cut across the board by 0.3 percent.

○ He has now signed a binding agreement to sell his 82 percent stake in the company.

al|lo|cate /æ̱ləkeɪt/ (allocates, allocated, allocating)

BASIC

VERB If you **allocate** funds, you divide up or distribute them.

○ Costs relating to the purchase of materials may be allocated according to the number of purchase transactions which have occurred.

○ The government will allocate some money in the budget each year to service this debt.

A

al|lo|ca|tion /ˈæləkeɪʃən/ (allocations)

MANAGEMENT

NOUN An **allocation** is an amount of money that is given to a particular person or used for a particular purpose.

○ If any of the committees doesn't meet its reduction target, its budget allocation would be cut across the board.

○ Start-of-the-year allocations made by foreign institutional investors can explain only part of the boom.

al|low|ance for bad debts /əˈlaʊəns fər bæd dɛts/

FINANCIAL STATEMENTS: BALANCE SHEET

NOUN **Allowance for bad debt** is a provision made in a company's accounts which recognizes that some debts will not be able to be collected.

○ When a bad debt occurs, it is written off the customer's account and charged against the allowance for bad debt.

○ The allowance for bad debt is the amount that the company estimates it will not be able to collect from customers.

▶ SYNONYMS:
allowance for doubtful accounts
allowance for uncollectibles

a|mor|ti|za|tion /ˌæmərtɪˈzeɪʃən/

BASIC

NOUN **Amortization** is a situation in which the value of intangible assets such as patents falls because of their age or how much they have been used.

○ This figure represents operating profit before depreciation and amortization.

○ The purpose of amortization is to reflect resale or redemption value.

a|mount /əˈmaʊnt/ (amounts)

BASIC

NOUN The **amount of** something is how much of it there is.

○ The amount of money available for reducing debt and debt service isn't finally set.

○ By lowering the level of corporation tax, the government should encourage more investment by business as companies are able to retain a larger amount of profit.

---

an|nu|al re|port /ˈænyuəl rɪpɔrt/ (**annual reports**)

FINANCIAL STATEMENTS

NOUN An **annual report** is a report that the directors of a company present to its stockholders each year.

○ The financial statement section of our most recent annual report is 32 pages long.

○ The annual report tells you what the company did last year, and how good its finances are.

A|P|R /eɪ pi ɑr/ (short for **annual percentage rate**)

BASIC

ABBREVIATION **APR** is the annual cost of a loan, including interest, insurance, and the original fee.

○ Shoppers with store credit cards could be paying an APR of as much as 30 percent.

○ Interest on the 9-month marketing loan has a current rate at 3.125 percent APR.

> **PRONUNCIATION**
>
> Three-letter abbreviations are usually pronounced as separate letters with the stress on the last syllable.
> **APR** /eɪ pi ɑr/
> **CIF** /si aɪ ɛf/
> **EFT** /i ɛf ti/
> **LLC** /ɛl ɛl si/

---

as|set ac|count /ˈæsɛt əkaʊnt/

FINANCIAL STATEMENTS: BALANCE SHEET

NOUN An **asset account** is an account that records the assets owned by a company.

○ Capital expenditures are debited to an asset account, and the expenditure is said to be capitalized.

○ The asset account increases with the amount of the assets that the owner brought into the business.

---

as|sets /ǽsɛts/

FINANCIAL STATEMENTS

NOUN The **assets** of a company or a person are all the things that they own.

○ A provisional liquidator can either restructure the company or sell off its assets.

○ The proportion of all luxury spending that went on art increased as investors looked for assets that would hold their value in the longer term.

> **RELATED WORDS**
>
> An organization's **assets** are the things it owns, and its **liabilities** are the sums of money that it owes. These sums are entered as claims on the assets shown on the balance sheet.

---

as|set turn|o|ver ra|ti|o /ǽsɛt tɜ́rnoʊvər reɪʃoʊ/
(**asset turnover ratios**)

MANAGEMENT

NOUN An **asset turnover ratio** is a measure of the efficiency of a company, that is calculated by dividing sales for a period by average total assets.

○ The higher the asset turnover ratio, the more efficiently the company uses its assets to generate sales.

○ The asset turnover ratio, which is a measure of how efficiently the assets of the company are used to generate sales, rose 5 percent.

▶ **SYNONYM:**
asset utilization ratio

au|dit¹ /ɔdɪt/ (audits)

FINANCIAL STATEMENTS

NOUN An **audit** is an inspection of business accounts that is carried out by an accountant in order to make sure that they are correct.

○ *Accountants have conducted an audit of the company, and uncovered the accounting discrepancies.*

○ *The regulator would reserve the right to declare a bank solvent after an audit.*

au|dit² /ɔdɪt/ (audits, audited, auditing)

FINANCIAL STATEMENTS

VERB When an accountant **audits** business accounts, he or she examines them officially in order to make sure that they are correct.

○ *Each year they audit our accounts and certify them as being true and fair.*

○ *The company's taxes for the years involved in the controversy are currently being audited.*

au|di|tor /ɔdɪtər/ (auditors)

FINANCIAL STATEMENTS

NOUN An **auditor** is an accountant who officially examines the accounts of organizations.

○ *An inquiry by the company's auditors revealed a series of incorrect accounting entries over several years.*

○ *Auditors judged that if the transaction went ahead the company would become technically insolvent.*

au|dit trail /ɔdɪt treɪl/

FINANCIAL STATEMENTS

NOUN An **audit trail** is the evidence, such as purchase orders and invoices, that a financial transaction actually occurred.

○ *They lack an audit trail, which would allow the regulatory agencies to reconstruct the sequence of trades.*

○ *An electronic audit trail of transactions would strengthen market regulations in many ways.*

Bb

---

bad debt /bæd dɛt/ (bad debts)

COMMERCE

NOUN A **bad debt** is a sum of money that a person or company owes but is not likely to pay back.

○ *The bank set aside 1.1 billion dollars to cover bad debts from business failures.*

○ *Bankruptcies have fallen sharply of late, which should slow the growth of bad debts on banks' books.*

---

bal|ance¹ /bæləns/ (balances)

FINANCIAL STATEMENTS

NOUN The **balance** of an account is the net amount at a particular time, including all credits and debits.

○ *The balance of an account refers to the amount in the account after recording increases and decreases.*

○ *The balances in the asset and liability accounts are used to prepare the financial statements.*

▶ SYNONYM:
acccount balance

---

bal|ance² /bæləns/ (balances, balanced, balancing)

FINANCIAL STATEMENTS

VERB If a business account or balance sheet **balances**, the debit and credit totals are equal.

○ *The balance sheet always balances because the purchase of assets must be financed out of either money raised from the business owners, or from money raised outside the business.*

○ *The account is designed to always balance, but the way that it is does so tells us how well a country is doing in its transactions with other countries.*

bal|ance an ac|count /bæləns ən əkaʊnt/

FINANCIAL STATEMENTS

PHRASE If you **balance an account**, you adjust entries in the account in order to make the credit and debit totals equal.

○ *If the growing new venture shows a profit, it is a fiction: a bookkeeping entry put in only to balance the accounts.*

○ *If that check is carried forward, you won't be able to balance the account at the end of the month.*

bal|anced score|card (ABBR **BS**) /bælənst skɔr kɑrd/ (**balanced scorecards**)

MANAGEMENT

NOUN A **balanced scorecard** is a type of management report which includes both financial and non-financial measures.

○ *The firm has used a balanced scorecard approach to management for the last five years, monitoring areas like product quality, staff and their satisfaction levels, client satisfaction, and financial performance.*

○ *Through the increasing use of techniques such as the balanced scorecard, companies were looking closely at their performance measures.*

bal|ance sheet /bæləns ʃit/ (**balance sheets**)

FINANCIAL STATEMENTS: BALANCE SHEET

NOUN A **balance sheet** is a statement of the amount of money and property that a company has and the amount of money that it owes.

○ *The strong currency has helped the balance sheets of Brazilian companies with international aspirations.*

○ *The company has improved its balance sheet during the past few years and begun making sizable payments to its underfunded pension-plan fund.*

bal|ance sheet ac|count /bæləns ʃit əkaʊnt/
(**balance sheet accounts**)

FINANCIAL STATEMENTS: BALANCE SHEET

NOUN A **balance sheet account** is an account in the chart of accounts that is reported on the balance sheet.

○ *The balance sheet accounts are the asset, liability, and owner's equity accounts.*

○ *Whether a deferral or an accrual, each adjustment will affect a balance sheet account and an income statement account.*

bal|ance sheet e|qua|tion /bæləns ʃit ɪkweɪʒⁿn/

FINANCIAL STATEMENTS: BALANCE SHEET

NOUN A **balance sheet equation** is a basic accounting equation that states that assets equal liabilities plus equity.

○ *The balance sheet equation states that the sum of the assets should equal the sum of the liabilities plus the capital invested.*

○ *The accounting model for the measurement of value and income is structured by the double-entry principle through what is known as the balance sheet equation.*

▶ **SYNONYM:**
accounting equation

bank /bæŋk/ (**banks**)

BASIC

NOUN A **bank** is a place or organization that looks after people's money.

○ *The company applied to the bank for a loan.*

○ *Students should look to see which bank offers them the service that best suits their financial needs.*

bank ac|count /bæŋk əkaʊnt/ (**bank accounts**)

COMMERCE

NOUN A **bank account** is an arrangement with a bank that allows you to keep your money in the bank and to take some out when you need it.

○ *The loans were backed by letters of credit secured by deposits in Swiss bank accounts.*

○ With point-of-sale debit cards, funds are electronically transferred out of a consumer's bank account at the time of purchase.

bank rec|on|cil|i|a|tion /bæŋk rɛkənsɪlieɪʃᵊn/
(bank reconciliations)

COMMERCE

COUNT/NONCOUNT NOUN A **bank reconciliation** is the process of adjusting a bank statement to show transactions that have occurred since the date of issue, or a document showing this.

○ The total deficit, as adjusted for bank reconciliation items, amounted to approximately $9,800,000.

○ The auditor needs to see the bank reconciliations for the past three months.

bank|rupt|cy /bæŋkrʌptsi/

BASIC

NOUN **Bankruptcy** is a legal recognition that a person, organization, or company does not have sufficient assets to repay its debts.

○ It is the second airline in two months to file for bankruptcy.

○ With the deepening recession, the number of corporate bankruptcies climbed in August.

bank state|ment /bæŋk steɪtmənt/ **(bank statements)**

COMMERCE

NOUN A **bank statement** is a document showing all the money paid into and taken out of a bank account during a particular period of time.

○ All transactions must appear on the next bank statement.

○ Online banking means that you can check your account balance before your monthly bank statement arrives in the mail.

be|gin|ning in|ven|to|ry /bəgɪnɪŋ ɪnvᵊntɔri/ **(beginning inventories)**

MANAGEMENT

NOUN A **beginning inventory** is all of the goods, services, or materials

B

that a business has available for use or sale at the start of a new accounting period.

○ *If the beginning inventory is overstated, cost of goods sold will be overstated and net income understated.*

○ *The cost of the ending inventory is larger than the cost of the beginning inventory because the firm bought more than it sold.*

---

be|low the line /bɪloʊ ðə laɪn/

FINANCIAL STATEMENTS: INCOME STATEMENT

ADJECTIVE **Below the line** income or expenses are entries that appear below a horizontal line on a company's profit and loss account, and show how the profit is to be distributed.

○ *The difference between exceptional and extraordinary items is unclear, because so many firms push costs below the line and pull revenues above it.*

○ *These items are placed below the line because they do not affect the value of the excess of revenues over expenses.*

---

bill¹ /bɪl/ (bills)

COMMERCE

NOUN A **bill** is a request for payment by a seller for goods or services provided.

○ *The company could no longer afford to pay their bills.*

○ *The group acquires companies and pays the takeover bill by selling the target's assets.*

---

bill² /bɪl/ (bills, billed, billing)

COMMERCE

VERB If you **bill** someone **for** goods or services, you send them a bill stating how much money they owe you.

○ *Are you going to bill me for this?*

○ *The company deliberately billed us for storage of items that have been out of the company's hands for up to three months.*

billable /bɪləbªl/

BASIC

ADJECTIVE **Billable** hours are the hours that a professional, especially a lawyer, spends doing work for clients, and for which the clients will have to pay.

○ Most law firms expect at least forty billable hours a week.

○ If a broker spends one hour in conference with you, or one hour with a seller, that clearly is billable time.

▶ **COLLOCATIONS:**
billable hours
billable time

bill of lad|ing /bɪl əv leɪdɪŋ/ (**bills of lading**)

COMMERCE

NOUN A **bill of lading** is a document containing full details of goods that are being transported by ship.

○ The bill of lading is issued by the carrier, and shows that the carrier has originated the shipment of merchandise.

○ The bill of lading is forwarded to the importer for the goods to be released.

bill of sale /bɪl əv seɪl/ (**bills of sale**)

COMMERCE

NOUN A **bill of sale** is a document sent by a seller to a purchaser that includes full details of the transaction.

○ The company executed a bill of sale under which they sold the assets of the restaurant and the goodwill of the franchised business.

○ He sold the merchandise for $1,800.00, but there is no bill of sale or any other document representing the sale.

board of di|rec|tors /bɔrd əv dɪrɛktərz/

MANAGEMENT

NOUN A company's **board of directors** is the group of people elected by the company's shareholders to manage the company.

○ The board of directors has approved the decision unanimously.

○ The board of directors has not yet decided whether a sale of the company is in the best interest of the company's shareholders and other constituencies.

---

bond /bɒnd/ (bonds)

INVESTING

NOUN A **bond** is a certificate issued to investors when a government or company borrows money from them.

○ The new credit, which the country will raise through issuing bonds to participating bank creditors, could total as much as $1.2 billion.

○ Bond prices strengthened yesterday as investors began to suspect that the Federal Reserve has once again eased credit policy.

---

bo|nus /boʊnəs/ (bonuses)

BASIC

NOUN A **bonus** is an extra amount of money that is paid to shareholders out of profits, or that is given to employees.

○ Each member of staff received a $100 bonus.

○ Savings holders may receive a cash bonus of as much as 75 cents a share.

---

book /bʊk/ (books, booked, booking)

FINANCIAL STATEMENTS

VERB If you **book** revenue, profit, or losses, you record or recognize them in a particular accounting period.

○ The executives were accused of improperly deferring expenses and booking revenue early, in an effort to improve results.

○ The way the company accounts for long-term contracts is often to book a profit on the sale for income that will be received only over many years.

▶ COLLOCATIONS:
book a loss
book a profit
book revenue

b

book de|pre|ci|a|tion /bʊk dɪpriːʃieɪʃˀn/

FINANCIAL STATEMENTS

NOUN **Book depreciation** is depreciation in a company's internal
financial records that is different from the amount that is used for taxes.

○ We can't ask accountants to recalculate each asset's present value every time
income is calculated, but we can ask them to match book depreciation
schedules to typical patterns of economic depreciation.

○ When tax depreciation exceeds book depreciation in the early years of
property life, deferred taxes are charged to expense with a contra credit to
a liability account.

book|keep|ing /bʊkkiːpɪŋ/

BASIC

NOUN **Bookkeeping** is the job or activity of keeping an accurate record
of the money that is spent and received by a business or other
organization.

○ The company's bookkeeping must follow certain strict principles, their books
are subject to periodic inspection, and they must make certain information
available to the public.

○ Accounts are separate bookkeeping records kept for each individual item in
the asset, liability, equity, revenue, and expense classifications.

books /bʊks/

BASIC

NOUN A company's **books** are its financial records.

○ If equity accounting has been followed, then the stated amount in the
investing company books will be cost plus retained profits.

○ The $2,500 fine was for failing to compute the company's net capital at least
once a month and to keep accurate books and records.

book-to-tax rec|on|cil|i|a|tion /bʊk tə tæks
rɛkənsɪlieɪʃˀn/ (**book-to-tax reconciliations**)

FINANCIAL STATEMENTS

NOUN A **book-to-tax reconciliation** is the act of reconciling the net income on the books to the income reported on the tax return by adding and subtracting the non-tax items.

○ *In performing a book-to-tax reconciliation, you must identify those items of income and deduction which differ from book to tax.*

○ *The tax exempt income is simply subtracted from book income in the book-to-tax reconciliation.*

---

book val|ue /bʊk vælyu/

FINANCIAL STATEMENTS

NOUN **Book value** is the value of a business asset as shown on the company's account books.

○ *The book value may understate current value or replacement cost.*

○ *The insured value of the airplane was greater than its book value.*

---

break e|ven /breɪk ivᵊn/ (breaks even, broke even, broken even, breaking even)

MANAGEMENT

VERB If a company **breaks even**, the money that it makes from the sale of goods or services is equal to the money that it has spent, so that there is neither profit nor loss.

○ *After last year's loss, he hopes to break even next year and post profits after that.*

○ *The company, which has never made a profit, has predicted it could break even if it could reach a workload of 150 cases a week.*

---

break|e|ven point /breɪkivᵊn pɔɪnt/

MANAGEMENT

NOUN **Breakeven point** is the point at which the money that a company makes from the sale of goods or services is equal to the money that it has spent, so that there is neither profit nor loss.

○ *They had to become a more efficient, lower-cost operation, which meant downsizing the company just to reduce their breakeven point.*

○ *Having cut staff numbers, we focused on reducing our inventory, lowering our breakeven point, and boosting our gross margins.*

bring for|ward /brɪŋ fɔrwəd/ (**brings forward, brought forward, bringing forward**)

BASIC

VERB If you **bring forward** a balance, you transfer it from a previous page or column of an account, or from another ledger or book, so that it will be the starting figure on a new page.

○ *The balance brought forward is the amount outstanding from the previous bill.*

○ *When a new page is started during a month, the totals of the Cash Credit columns are brought forward from the previous page.*

bring o|ver /brɪŋ oʊvər/ (**brings over, brought over, bringing over**)

BASIC

VERB If you **bring over** or **bring down** a balance, you transfer it from the previous accounting period to the current one.

○ *Most of the current assets are not adjusted for the new accounting period, and are simply brought over at their recorded amounts.*

○ *The balance brought down from last year was $35,160.*

▶ SYNONYM:
 bring down

budg|et¹ /bʌdʒɪt/ (**budgets**)

MANAGEMENT

NOUN The **budget** of an organization is its financial situation, considered as the difference between the money that it expects to receive and the money that it expects to spend over a particular period.

○ *The final effect of all the planning is reflected in the statement of planned financial position at the close of the budget period.*

○ *The budget for the financial year was originally planned to bring down the fiscal deficit to around 5 percent of the GDP.*

budg|et² /bʌdʒɪt/ (**budgets**)

MANAGEMENT

NOUN A **budget** is the total amount of money allocated for a particular purpose during a particular period of time.

○ The company's R&D budget, which is about $125 million this year, may have to be doubled in a few years.

○ Last year the company launched a new product with only 25 percent of its advertising budget allocated to TV.

---

budg|et³ /bʌdʒɪt/ (budgets, budgeted, budgeting)

BASIC

VERB If you **budget**, you allocate certain amounts of money to particular things and do not spend any more.

○ The stress of debt can be overcome by people learning how to budget.

○ Children need to understand that they are part of the economics of the family, and should learn how to budget and make decisions.

---

budg|et⁴ /bʌdʒɪt/ (budgets, budgeted, budgeting)

BASIC

VERB If you **budget** a certain amount of money **for** something, you decide that you can spend that amount.

○ The company has budgeted $10 million for advertising.

○ The country has budgeted $1.7 billion for wheat subsidies this year.

---

budg|et for /bʌdʒɪt fɔr/ (budgets for, budgeted for, budgeting for)

BASIC

VERB If you **budget for** a particular purpose or period of time, you allocate, save, or set aside certain amounts of money for that purpose or period.

○ The plan is to redevelop the area into a business center of high-tech buildings, a project budgeted for 30 years and six trillion yen.

○ The annual advertising spend would be budgeted for at the beginning of the year.

Cc

---

cal|en|dar year /kælɪndər yɪər/ (calendar years)

BASIC

NOUN A **calendar year** is a business year that goes from January 1 to December 31.

- ○ In the last calendar year, the company had a turnover of $426m.
- ○ Comparable year-ago figures are not available because the company switched to a calendar year from a Jan. 31 fiscal year.

C & F /siː ənd ɛf/ (short for **cost & freight**)

COMMERCE

ABBREVIATION **C & F** refers to a shipping contract which includes the cost of the goods and the freight, but not insurance.

- ○ With a C & F contract, the price of the goods includes the cost of the goods and the freight to the named destination.
- ○ We're sending the shipment C&F destination.

---

cap|i|tal /kæpɪtᵊl/

INVESTING

NOUN **Capital** is money that you use to start a business.

- ○ They provide capital for the start-up of small businesses.
- ○ Companies are having difficulty in raising capital.

WORD FAMILY

capital NOUN ○ They were trying to raise the capital to buy the building outright.

> **capitalization** NOUN ○ *The company had shed $240 billion in market capitalization since its peak.*
>
> **capitalize** VERB ○ *In some cooperatives, members reinvest their earnings to capitalize the business.*

---

cap|i|tal ac|count /ˈkæpɪtᵊl əˈkaʊnt/ (capital accounts)

FINANCIAL STATEMENTS: BALANCE SHEET

NOUN A **capital account** is an account that shows the net value of a company.

○ *The proprietor's capital account now has a net credit balance of $10,550.*

○ *The capital account is the equity account that shows a sole proprietor's or partner's investment in the business.*

---

cap|i|tal ex|pense /ˈkæpɪtᵊl ɪksˈpɛns/ (capital expenses)

FINANCIAL STATEMENTS

NOUN A **capital expense** is the cost of acquiring or making improvements to fixed assets.

○ *Under a private-finance initiative deal, a private consortium raises money to fund the capital expense of a new hospital.*

○ *The investment in new technology was a one-time capital expense while the costs of operating an additional workstation would be recurring.*

---

cap|i|tal gain¹ /ˈkæpɪtᵊl ˈgeɪn/ (capital gains)

FINANCIAL STATEMENTS

NOUN A **capital gain** is the amount by which the selling price of a financial asset exceeds its cost.

○ *A capital gain is the increase in the market value of an asset.*

○ *The sale of shares for withdrawal payments constitutes a taxable event and a shareholder may incur a capital gain for federal income tax purposes.*

---

cap|i|tal gain² /ˈkæpɪtᵊl ˈgeɪn/ (capital gains)

TAX

NOUN A **capital gain** is a gain on investment property.

○ The net cost of buying includes interest payments on a 90 percent mortgage, plus annual maintenance costs of 1.5 percent of the value of the property, minus the capital gain on the apartment.

○ Without a guaranteed capital gain, the advantage of buying a home over renting narrows significantly.

---

cap|i|tal|i|za|tion /ˌkæpɪtᵊlɪˈzeɪʃᵊn/ (**capitalizations**)

INVESTING

NOUN A **capitalization** is the sum of the total share capital issued by a company.

○ The company's market capitalization has fallen from $650 million to less than $60 million.

○ The venture will have initial capitalization of one billion yen and will spend 15 billion yen to build the plant.

---

cap|i|tal|ize¹ /ˈkæpɪtᵊlaɪz/ (**capitalizes, capitalized, capitalizing**)

INVESTING

VERB If you **capitalize** a business enterprise, you obtain money from somewhere to start or run your business.

○ We can capitalize the business by borrowing money, looking for private investment, or issuing stock.

○ We have found an investor who will capitalize the new bank with about $15 million.

▶ **COLLOCATION:**
capitalize a business

---

cap|i|tal|ize² /ˈkæpɪtᵊlaɪz/ (**capitalizes, capitalized, capitalizing**)

FINANCIAL STATEMENTS

VERB If you **capitalize** a purchase, you treat it as an asset rather than an expense.

○ Rather than expense the purchase of the new computer, we decided to capitalize it and keep it on the balance sheet as an asset.

○ The Tax Court told the company that the takeover expense must be capitalized.

▶ COLLOCATIONS:
capitalize a purchase
capitalize an expense

---

cap|i|tal lease /kæpɪtᵊl lis/ (capital leases)

FINANCIAL STATEMENTS

NOUN A **capital lease** is a lease which is treated as the purchase of the asset that is being leased.

○ *A capital lease is thus more like a purchase or sale on installment than a rental.*

○ *Under accounting rules, a capital lease is treated like a purchase.*

---

cap|i|tal loss /kæpɪtᵊl lɔs/ (capital losses)

TAX

NOUN A **capital loss** is a loss on investment property.

○ *The fund receives additional income, in the form of a premium, which may offset any capital loss or decline in market value of the security.*

○ *The yield on the benchmark ten-year bond has increased from a low of 2.98 percent on January 7th to 3.43 percent on February 9th, creating a capital loss to investors of 3.4 percent.*

---

cap|i|tal stock /kæpɪtᵊl stɒk/

INVESTING

NOUN A company's **capital stock** is the money that stockholders invest in order to start or expand the business.

○ *The bank has a capital stock of almost 100 million dollars.*

○ *R&D spending is not shown as capital in their accounts, so that their capital stock is really higher than it appears.*

---

car|ry back /kæri bæk/ (carries back, carried back, carrying back)

TAX

VERB If you **carry back** a loss or credit, you apply it to a previous tax year.

○ *The legislation will reduce the amount of losses that can be carried back for tax purposes by corporations that replace equity with debt.*

○ *A net operating loss must first be carried back to the third year preceding the year in which it was sustained.*

RELATED WORDS
Phrasal verbs

There are several phrasal verbs that are commonly used in bookkeeping. **Carry back** means to apply an amount to a previous tax year, **bring over** relates to bringing an amount from the previous to the current period, while **carry forward** and **carry over** relate to bringing amounts from the current to the next period.

If you **set off** a debit from one account against credit from another, you deduct it. If you **write down** an asset, you decrease its book value, and if you **write off** a bad debt, you cancel it from the accounts.

---

car|ry for|ward¹ /kǽri fɔ́rwərd/ (carries forward, carried forward, carrying forward)

BASIC

VERB If you **carry forward** a balance, you transfer it to the next page or column of an account, or to another ledger or book, so that it will be the starting figure there.

○ *This balance is carried forward from the previous page.*

○ *Is the client's current balance carried forward to the next billing?*

---

car|ry for|ward² /kǽri fɔ́rwərd/ (carries forward, carried forward, carrying forward)

TAX

VERB If you **carry forward** a loss or credit, you apply it to a following tax year.

○ *It is extremely rare for advertising and market research expenditure to be carried forward; it is generally written off in the year in which it is incurred.*

○ *The balance sheet's asset, liability, and owner's equity balances are permanent running totals that are carried forward to the next accounting year.*

car|ry|ing charge /ˈkæriɪŋ tʃɑrdʒ/ (carrying charges)

MANAGEMENT

NOUN A **carrying charge** is the opportunity cost of unproductive assets, such as goods stored in a warehouse.

○ *The contract is to purchase the air conditioners and to sell them on an installment plan with collections over approximately 30 months with no carrying charge.*

○ *The price will reflect this excess in the cost of interest, and the carrying charge of storing and insuring the goods for another 60 or 90 days or so.*

car|ry o|ver /ˈkæri ˈoʊvər/ (carries over, carried over, carrying over)

BASIC

VERB If you **carry over**, **carry down**, or **carry** a balance, you transfer it to the next accounting period, where it will be the opening balance.

○ *Any balance in the factory overhead account should not be carried over to the next year.*

○ *Any unspent balance carried over to next year has to be reallocated.*

▶ **SYNONYMS:**
carry
carry down

cash /kæʃ/

BASIC

NOUN **Cash** is money in the form of bills and coins.

○ *Are you paying by cash, check, or card?*

○ *They paid us $2000 in cash.*

cash ba|sis /kæʃ ˈbeɪsɪs/

FINANCIAL STATEMENTS

NOUN A **cash basis** is a system of accounting where income is recognized when it is received, and expenses when they are paid.

○ *Using the cash basis of accounting, the firm records sales as it receives cash.*

○ *Only buy on a cash basis. If you can't afford something, save up for it.*

cash book /kæʃ bʊk/ (**cash books**)

FINANCIAL STATEMENTS: INCOME STATEMENT

NOUN A **cash book** is a book in which all cash or check receipts and expenditure are recorded.

○ The cash book records all receipts, and is reconciled to the bank statements.

○ The cash book should show the amounts received on a daily basis and should also record all cash payments, and be balanced regularly.

cash dis|count /kæʃ dɪskaʊnt/ (**cash discounts**)

COMMERCE

NOUN A **cash discount** is a reduction in price that is given to a purchaser who pays in cash or before a particular date.

○ Are you prepared to offer a cash discount for prompt payment?

○ Goods may be sold on terms which allow the customer a cash discount of 8 percent if the bill is paid within 10 days of the end of month.

cash flow /kæʃ floʊ/ (**cash flows**)

FINANCIAL STATEMENTS

NOUN The **cash flow** of a business is the movement of money into and out of it.

○ The company ran into cash flow problems and faced liquidation.

○ Instead of massive investment, they have to finance growth from cash flow, which makes them concentrate on profits.

C cor|po|ra|tion /si kɔrpəreɪʃⁿn/ (**C corporations**)

BASIC

NOUN A **C corporation** is a type of corporation which is taxed on its income.

○ As a C corporation, we have to pay taxes of 39 percent on the portion of our annual earnings between $100,000 and $335,000.

○ When a tax return is filed for a C-corporation, the corporation pays taxes on the net profit of the business.

charge¹ /tʃɑrdʒ/ (charges, charged, charging)

COMMERCE

VERB If you **charge** someone, you ask them to pay an amount of money for something that you have sold to them or done for them.

○ The federal funds rate is the interest rate that banks charge one another for short-term loans.

○ The architect charged us a fee of $750.

charge² /tʃɑrdʒ/ (charges)

FINANCIAL STATEMENTS: BALANCE SHEET

NOUN A **charge** is an amount of money that you have to pay for something.

○ We can arrange this for a small charge.

○ Instead of the contractors imposing charges on motorists, their revenues will depend on the numbers of vehicles using the route.

charge³ /tʃɑrdʒ/ (charges)

FINANCIAL STATEMENTS: BALANCE SHEET

NOUN A **charge** is a debt or a book entry that records a debt.

○ The entry for the charge for insurance is made in the journal.

○ The company took a restructuring charge of $949m, mostly to cover closures and 7,000 job losses in chemicals.

charge|back /tʃɑrdʒbæk/ (chargebacks)

COMMERCE

COUNT/NONCOUNT NOUN A **chargeback** is the act of charging a cost back to an account.

○ If someone has paid money into the account and not received the goods, under what is called a chargeback, the company can take money from the seller's account and return it to the buyer.

○ Assuming you paid by credit card, the best way to get a refund is to reclaim the money via a chargeback.

chart of ac|counts /tʃɑrt əv əkaʊnts/ (**charts of accounts**)

FINANCIAL STATEMENTS

NOUN A **chart of accounts** is a list of all the accounts used in a business to classify transactions or report balances.

○ Your chart of accounts is the list of accounts that you maintain to keep track of revenue, expense, assets, and liabilities.

○ Your chart of accounts is the backbone of your business, to accurately code where your dollars are spent so you can make the most of your business' tax savings.

check¹ /tʃɛk/ (**checks, checked, checking**)

BASIC

VERB If you **check** something, you make sure that it is correct.

○ You should keep a record of what you spend and check it against bank statements.

○ Check the accuracy of all the figures in the profit and loss account.

check² /tʃɛk/ (**checks**)

COMMERCE

NOUN A **check** is a printed form from a bank that you write on and use to pay for things. Your bank then pays the money from your account.

○ He paid me with a check for $1,500.

○ The funds allow shareholders to redeem shares by writing checks above $500 on the fund's account at a commercial bank.

check|ing ac|count /tʃɛkɪŋ əkaʊnt/ (**checking accounts**)

COMMERCE

NOUN A **checking account** is a bank account that you can take money out of by writing a check.

○ Do not mix business and personal finances by using the same checking account for your home and business.

○ He has his checking account at the Commonwealth Bank.

C

check reg|is|ter /tʃɛk redʒɪstər/ (**check registers**)

COMMERCE

NOUN A **check register** is a record of transactions in a checking account.

○ *Keep track of how much money you have in your checking account by recording checks and other transactions in your check register.*

○ *Verify the signature on the back of the cleared check and verify that the name and amount on the check agrees with the check register.*

check stub /tʃɛk stʌb/ (**check stubs**)

COMMERCE

NOUN A **check stub** is the part of a check that is kept by the payee with information such as the check number, date, and amount.

○ *If you accurately record on your check stubs what you have paid out, you should build up a very accurate account of your finances.*

○ *A check stub is a business's record of each check written for a cash payment transaction.*

C|I|F /siː aɪ ɛf/ (short for **cost, insurance and freight**)

COMMERCE

ABBREVIATION **CIF** refers to a shipping contract which includes the cost of goods, insurance, and freight.

○ *CIF values include the transaction value of the goods and the value of the services performed to deliver the goods from the border of the exporting country to the border of the importing country.*

○ *They fixed a higher price of $178.75 a tonne on a CIF basis for supply of wheat to India.*

clas|si|fy /klæsɪfaɪ/ (**classifies, classified, classifying**)

FINANCIAL STATEMENTS

VERB If you **classify** things, you divide them into groups or types.

○ *They are classified as limited liability companies.*

○ *Under the present system, bank assets are classified into 4 broad risk categories.*

clear /klɪər/
BASIC

ADJECTIVE **Clear** profits are profits without any deduction.

- ○ If the warrants are never exercised, the proceeds from their sale will become a clear profit to the company.
- ○ The company's outgoings and revenues balanced out, leaving investment income as clear profit.

close out /kloʊz aʊt/ (closes out, closed out, closing out)
BASIC

VERB If you **close out** an account on which the margin is inadequate or exhausted, you terminate it, usually by selling securities to realize cash.

- ○ The debit to sales revenue and the credits to expenses close out these accounts.
- ○ He would also close out or set to zero all the revenue and expense accounts for the year in preparation for recording the next year's activity in the following entry.

close the books /kloʊz ðə bʊks/
FINANCIAL STATEMENTS

PHRASE If you **close the books**, you balance accounts in order to prepare a statement or report. It can also informally be used as a noun: "the close."

- ○ Accountants want to be able to close the books with a positive result against any negative expense.
- ○ As the system still doesn't track inventory well, in order to close the books on its June quarter, the company must now finish some of the accounting work by hand.

C|O|D /si oʊ di/ (short for **cash on delivery**)
COMMERCE

ABBREVIATION **COD** is used to describe payment terms by which cash is paid when goods or services are delivered.

○ If you are supplying goods to a wide variety of irregular customers, you may require COD.

○ Customers quickly get used to the idea of ordering products on the Net, paying with their credit cards or through COD, and having the products delivered to their doorsteps.

---

col|lat|er|al /kəlǽtərəl/

INVESTING

NOUN **Collateral** is money or property which is used as a guarantee that someone will repay a loan.

○ Many people use personal assets as collateral for small business loans.

○ He agreed to lend the company $40 million, using its substantial assets as collateral.

---

col|lect /kəlɛkt/ (collects, collected, collecting)

COMMERCE

VERB If you **collect**, or **collect on** a debt, you receive payment on a debt.

○ The company hasn't yet tried to collect on the outstanding balance.

○ In recent months, difficulties in collecting Third World loans have mounted.

---

com|mis|sion /kəmɪʃ°n/

COMMERCE

NOUN **Commission** is payment of part of the revenues or profits from a sale or deal that is paid to the person who arranged or facilitated the deal.

○ Travel agents charge 1 percent commission on tickets.

○ The salespeople work on commission only.

---

com|mon stock /kɒmən stɒk/

INVESTING

NOUN **Common stock** refers to the shares in a company that are owned by people who have a right to receive part of the company's profits after the holders of preferred stock have been paid.

○ The company priced its offering of 2.7 million shares of common stock at 20 cents a share.

○ The banking concern said that under the plan, shareholders will exchange their common stock for an equal number of shares in the new holding company.

---

com|pen|sa|tion /kɒmpənseɪʃ³n/
BASIC

NOUN **Compensation** is money that someone who has experienced inconvenience, loss, or suffering claims from the person or organization responsible, or from the state.

○ He has to pay $6,960 compensation for the damage he caused.

○ The basic award is calculated in the same way as redundancy compensation on each full year of service in various brackets.

---

com|pound in|ter|est /kɒmpaʊnd ɪntrɪst/
INVESTING

NOUN **Compound interest** is interest that is paid both on an original sum of money and on interest that has already been paid on that sum.

○ When money is invested at compound interest, each interest payment is reinvested to earn more interest in subsequent periods.

○ We compute compound interest on principal and on any interest earned that has not been paid or withdrawn.

---

con|sign|ment /kənsaɪnmənt/
COMMERCE

NOUN **Consignment** is the act of leaving goods with someone else to sell while retaining ownership until the goods are sold.

○ Goods are sometimes supplied on a consignment basis, so that payment is not made until after the buyer has sold the goods, and in the meantime the goods remain the property of the supplier.

○ When a manufacturer supplies goods to a dealer on consignment, the dealer can return the goods without incurring a loss.

C

con|tra ac|count /ˈkɒntrə əˈkaʊnt/ (**contra accounts**)

FINANCIAL STATEMENTS

NOUN A **contra account** is an account with a balance that is the opposite of the normal balance of a related account.

○ *An account that reduces a related account is known as a contra account.*

○ *Book depreciation is the contra account to the asset that is being depreciated on the balance sheet.*

con|tract /ˈkɒntrækt/ (**contracts**)

COMMERCE

NOUN A **contract** is an official agreement between two or more companies or people, in which each party has rights and obligations.

○ *They recently signed a contract with a major food company to supply a billion aluminum food cans.*

○ *Producers are refusing to sign long-term contracts because they expect higher prices.*

> **TALKING ABOUT CONTRACTS**
>
> People **negotiate** a contract to come to an agreement, and when they have done that, they **sign** the contract.
>
> If you end a contract, you **terminate** or **cancel** it, and if the contract reaches the end of its time period, it **expires**. If you agree to make it longer, you **extend** it.

con|trol[1] /kənˈtroʊl/ (**controls, controlled, controlling**)

BASIC

VERB If you **control** financial affairs, you regulate them.

○ *By controlling all financial supervision, the commission would be in a much better position than today's regulators to judge when firms need assistance.*

○ *In the country's tightly controlled financial system, savers have little choice.*

con|trol² /kəntr<u>oʊ</u>l/ (**controls, controlled, controlling**)

FINANCIAL STATEMENTS

VERB If you **control** financial accounts, you examine them and check that they are correct.

- ○ *Large brokerage firms have knowledge of highly specialized insurance markets and control the accounts of large corporate insurance buyers.*
- ○ *Their lawyer controlled the account and the funds were disbursed from the account to discharge the company's financial obligations.*

con|trol ac|count /kəntr<u>oʊ</u>l əkaʊnt/ (**control accounts**)

FINANCIAL STATEMENTS

NOUN A **control account** is an account which contains the debit and credit totals of other accounts, and is used to prepare financial statements.

- ○ *A control account is a summary account, where entries are made from totals of transactions for a period.*
- ○ *The sum of the balances in the individual customers' accounts is the balance in the control account.*

cor|po|rate /kɔrpərɪt/

BASIC

ADJECTIVE **Corporate** means relating to large companies, or to a particular large company.

- ○ *Interest rates are higher for corporate clients than for private clients.*
- ○ *The economy is growing, and corporate profits are rising.*

cor|po|ra|tion /kɔrpəreɪʃᵊn/ (**corporations**)

BASIC

NOUN A **corporation** is a large business or company.

- ○ *The interests of management and shareholders often conflict, particularly when a corporation is subject to a possible takeover attempt.*
- ○ *The nation's largest corporations aren't directly affected by prime rate changes because many can borrow at rates well below the prime.*

C

cost /kɔst/ (costs, costed, costing)

MANAGEMENT

VERB If you **cost** or **cost out** a product or process, you estimate what it is going to cost, for the purposes of pricing or budgeting.

○ If we want to fully cost a particular product, for example, when we wish to set prices, we will need to know all the expenses connected with that product.

○ We need to cost out the project in order to see exactly how much money is required.

RELATED WORDS

Organizations have many different costs.

Costs involved in running a business, such as salaries, rent, and bills are known as **overhead**.

---

cost ac|count|ing /kɔst əkaʊntɪŋ/

MANAGEMENT

NOUN **Cost accounting** is the recording and analysis of all the various costs of running a business.

○ Traditional cost accounting measures what it costs to do something.

○ Cost accounting can help to improve the utilization of resources such as manpower, plant and machinery, vehicles, buildings, and cash.

▶ SYNONYMS:
management accounting
managerial accounting

---

cost cen|ter /kɔst sɛntər/ (cost centers)

MANAGEMENT

NOUN A **cost center** is a department in a company that does not bring the company direct profit.

○ Corporate education used merely to be a cost center; now it is considered as a potential profit center too.

○ They took what was historically a cost center and converted it into an independent and profitable entity.

cost of goods a|vail|a|ble for sale /kɔst əv gʊdz əveɪləbᵊl fər seɪl/

FINANCIAL STATEMENTS

NOUN The **cost of goods available for sale** is the cost of the raw materials and labor used to manufacture goods that a company has that are finished and ready and available to be sold.

○ When the cost of goods purchased is added to beginning inventory, the result is cost of goods available for sale.

○ The cost of goods available for sale is calculated by adding the beginning inventory and the amount of goods that have been purchased or manufactured.

cost of goods sold (ABBR COGS) /kɔst əv gʊdz soʊld/

FINANCIAL STATEMENTS: INCOME STATEMENT

NOUN The **cost of goods sold** is the cost of purchasing goods for resale, added to the cost of the raw materials and labor used to manufacture goods that are sold in a particular period of time.

○ The cost of goods sold is calculated as beginning inventory plus purchases plus materials and labor minus ending inventory.

○ The cost of goods sold on the income statement reflects all costs directly tied to any product a company sells, be it a merchandiser or a manufacturing company.

▶ **SYNONYM:**
cost of sales

cost o|ver|run /kɔst oʊvərrʌn/ (**cost overruns**)

MANAGEMENT

NOUN A **cost overrun** is a cost that is more than the amount budgeted.

○ To date they have spent $16 million on the project; however, expenditure was halted when the scale of the cost overrun became apparent.

○ The banks reportedly agreed to provide an additional $8 million to complete the hotel after the cost overrun emerged.

C

cov|er /kʌvər/ (covers, covered, covering)

BASIC

VERB If an asset or income **covers** a liability or expense, it is sufficient to pay the costs of the liability or expense.

○ *That sale will cover this month's rent.*

○ *Some of the company's large stock of assets are likely to be sold to cover the debts.*

C|P|A /si pi eɪ/ (short for **certified public accountant**)

BASIC

ABBREVIATION A **CPA** is a public accountant in the US who is certified to have met state legal requirements.

○ *Compared to an accounting graduate who has not yet attained certification, CPAs command higher salaries.*

○ *Nobody but a CPA can handle an audit and represent clients before the IRS.*

cred|it¹ /krɛdɪt/ (credits)

FINANCIAL STATEMENTS

NOUN A **credit** is an entry on the right-hand side of an account.

○ *In double entry bookkeeping, a transaction is recorded as a debit in one account and as a credit in another.*

○ *The entry for paying rent is a credit to the bank account and a debit to rent expense.*

> **RELATED WORDS**
>
> The opposite of **credit** is **debit**, both for the noun and for both senses of the verb.

cred|it² /krɛdɪt/ (credits, credited, crediting)

FINANCIAL STATEMENTS

VERB If you **credit** someone, or **credit** their account, you allocate money to their account.

○ *The customer sent in a check, so you must credit their account for the amount of the check.*

○ *As the goods you ordered arrived late, I'll credit you for the delivery charges.*

---

cred|it³ /krɛdɪt/ (credits, credited, crediting)

COMMERCE

VERB If you **credit** a sum of money to an account, you add that sum of money to the total in the account.

○ *The full premium is credited to the policy owner's account and earns interest immediately at the current interest rate.*

○ *Although profits are credited to the profit and loss account each year, no actual cash relating to these profits is taken out of the business until the end of the lease period.*

---

cred|it mem|o /krɛdɪt mɛmoʊ/ (credit memos)

COMMERCE

NOUN A **credit memo** is an official written acknowledgement that money is owed back to a customer.

○ *When you need to create a refund for a client, you can create a credit memo, which is basically an invoice with a negative amount.*

○ *A credit memo is necessary if a customer returns goods or has been billed for goods that were lost or damaged in shipment.*

---

cred|i|tor /krɛdɪtər/ (creditors)

COMMERCE

NOUN A **creditor** is an organization or person who people owe money to.

○ *The company said it would pay in full all its creditors.*

○ *A provisional liquidator can either restructure or liquidate assets and distribute proceeds to creditors.*

---

cred|it side /krɛdɪt saɪd/

FINANCIAL STATEMENTS

NOUN The **credit side** of an account is the right-hand side.

C

○ The transactions involving cash payments are listed on the credit side of the balance sheet.

○ In asset accounts, increases to assets are recorded on the debit side while decreases are recorded on the credit side.

---

cu|mu|la|tive /kyu̲myələtɪv/

BASIC

ADJECTIVE **Cumulative** dividends or earnings are added on from period to period.

○ Analysts estimate that third-quarter earnings for the industry will increase as much as 19 percent from the year-earlier period. If so, their cumulative earnings could hit $4.12 billion.

○ The Fund provided a six-month cumulative return of 3.26 percent for the six months ended August 31.

▶ COLLOCATIONS:
cumulative dividends
cumulative earnings
cumulative interest
cumulative profit

---

cur|rent /kɜrənt/

BASIC

ADJECTIVE **Current** means happening, being used, or being done at the present time, or expected to take place within a year or less.

○ Current expenditure exceeds the original estimate.

○ He recommends that investors hold up for the time being in buying the stock, as current profit margins probably aren't sustainable.

▶ SYNONYM:
short-term

---

cur|rent as|sets /kɜrənt æsɛts/

FINANCIAL STATEMENTS: BALANCE SHEET

NOUN **Current assets** are assets which a company has which can be converted into cash within one year.

○ *Examples of other current assets include property held for sale and advances or deposits.*

○ *Current assets include stock, money owed to the business by debtors, and cash.*

cur|rent cost /kɜrənt kɔst/ (current costs)

FINANCIAL STATEMENTS

NOUN The **current cost** of assets is their current value, or what it would cost to replace them at this time.

○ *The drawback to using the current cost rather than historical cost approach is that cost estimates may be difficult and costly to obtain.*

○ *The depreciation adjustment requires that the fixed assets included in the historical cost balance sheet be restated at their value to the business by reference to current costs.*

> **RELATED WORDS**
>
> Compare **current cost** to **historical cost**, which is the original cost of an asset when it was first acquired by a company.

cur|rent ex|pens|es /kɜrənt ɪkspɛnsɪz/

FINANCIAL STATEMENTS

NOUN **Current expenses** are the everyday costs in running a business for things that are used continually or will be used within one year.

○ *They deduct current expenses when calculating profit but do not deduct capital expenses.*

○ *Current expenses include the day-to-day costs of running your business, such as office supplies, rent, and electricity.*

cur|rent li|a|bil|i|ties /kɜrənt laɪəbɪlɪtiz/

FINANCIAL STATEMENTS: BALANCE SHEET

NOUN **Current liabilities** are debts that come due within a year.

○ *We are looking for a company whose current assets are at least twice their current liabilities.*

○ *The current liabilities of trade creditors, overdraft, and expense creditors will all make demands on the working capital within a year.*

cur|rent ra|ti|o /kɜrənt reɪʃoʊ/ (**current ratios**)

INVESTING

NOUN A **current ratio** is a measure of liquidity that is calculated by dividing current assets by current liabilities.

○ *The current ratio is a test of a business's short-term solvency: its capability to pay its liabilities that fall due within the next year.*

○ *A manufacturer normally needs a current ratio of around 2:1. More than this suggests poor resource usage and potential liquidity problems.*

▶ SYNONYM:
   working capital ratio

cus|tom|er /kʌstəmər/ (**customers**)

BASIC

NOUN A **customer** is someone who buys products or services.

○ *He introduced stricter measures for slow-paying customers and directed his sales staff to find new accounts.*

○ *Transaction fees are charged to customers who don't keep a certain minimum balance in their account.*

Dd

deb|it¹ /dɛbɪt/ (debits)

FINANCIAL STATEMENTS

NOUN A **debit** is an entry on the left-hand side of an account.

○ If there is a requirement for regular pension costs to be funded in full, the accounting entries are a credit to cash and a debit to regular pension costs.

○ The statement of total debits and credits is known as a trial balance.

deb|it² /dɛbɪt/ (debits, debited, debiting)

FINANCIAL STATEMENTS

VERB If you **debit** an account, you make an entry on the left side of the account.

○ The excess is debited to this account if it contains a sufficient credit balance to absorb this debit.

○ To record a cash sale, you credit sales revenue and debit the bank account.

deb|it³ /dɛbɪt/ (debits, debited, debiting)

COMMERCE

VERB If an item or a customer's account **is debited**, money is taken out of it to pay someone else.

○ When you charge your credit card, you credit the credit card account to increase the amount that you owe, and debit the expense that you charged on it.

○ The bank will debit your account for the fees.

D

deb|it side /dɛbɪt saɪd/

FINANCIAL STATEMENTS

NOUN The **debit side** of an account is the left-hand side.

○ This is the first item on the debit side of the account, that is discharged, or reduced, by the first item on the credit side.

○ An account is said to have a debit balance if the total of the debit side is greater than that of the credit side.

debt /dɛt/ (**debts**)

COMMERCE

NOUN A **debt** is an amount of money that you owe someone.

○ The company planned to use the proceeds from the sale to help pay the debt incurred in its proposed $12 billion acquisition.

○ The company is considering whether to sell other assets to reduce its debts.

> **PRONUNCIATION**
>
> Note the silent "b" in this word, and in the related word **debtor**.

debt|or /dɛtər/ (**debtors**)

COMMERCE

NOUN A **debtor** is an organization or person that owes money.

○ Any concession that creditors grant to one debtor would set a precedent for all the others.

○ When a business offers a customer credit for the purchase of a good or service, then that customer becomes a debtor of that business.

debt-to-eq|ui|ty ra|ti|o /dɛt tu ɛkwɪti reɪʃoʊ/ (**debt-to-equity ratios**)

INVESTING

NOUN A company's **debt-to-equity ratio** is a measure of leverage that is calculated by dividing total liabilities by shareholders' equity.

○ The debt-to-equity ratio reveals the proportion of debt and equity a company is using to finance its business.

○ *The debt-to-equity ratio indicates how the firm finances its operations with debt relative to the book value of its shareholders' equity.*

de|duc|tion /dɪdˈʌkʃ°n/ (deductions)

TAX

NOUN A **deduction** is an expense that can be deducted from income on a tax return.

○ *Most homeowners can get a federal income tax deduction on interest payments to a home equity loan.*

○ *Government aid to industry includes outright grants, low-interest loans, and tax incentives such as deductions.*

de|fault /dɪˈfɔlt/ (defaults, defaulted, defaulting)

BASIC

VERB If a person or organization **defaults on** a payment, they fail to pay an amount that they owe.

○ *Purchasers of bonds need to know whether a corporation is likely to default on its bonds.*

○ *The credit card business is down, and more borrowers are defaulting on loans.*

de|fer|ral /dɪˈfɜrəl/ (deferrals)

FINANCIAL STATEMENTS

NOUN A **deferral** is a transaction that will be recognized in a later accounting period.

○ *The longer you hold the asset and the higher the interest rate, the more the deferral is worth.*

○ *The group asked its 100 creditor banks for a two-year deferral of up to $1 billion of debt repayments.*

WORD FAMILY

deferral NOUN ○ *The balance for the rent is not covered by the deferral.*

deferred ADJECTIVE ○ *There was a reduction in the net deferred income tax asset of approximately $160 million.*

These words come from the verb **defer**, which means "to make something happen at a later time than originally planned."

---

de|ferred /dɪfɜrd/

FINANCIAL STATEMENTS

ADJECTIVE **Deferred** expenses are paid for before they are used, and **deferred** income is received before it has been earned.

○ *A deferred annuity provides an income at some future date.*

○ *Most companies hold large provisions for the payment of deferred taxation on their balance sheets.*

---

def|i|cit¹ /dɛfəsɪt/ (deficits)

BASIC

NOUN A **deficit** is a situation in which liabilities are greater than assets.

○ *Cash in-flows and out-flows must be balanced against each other, with a surplus placed on the asset side or a deficit on the liability side.*

○ *Slashing capital spending and selling off public assets reduce the budget deficit in the short term but do little to correct the underlying fiscal imbalance.*

---

def|i|cit² /dɛfəsɪt/ (deficits)

BASIC

NOUN A **deficit** is a situation in which expenses are greater than revenues during a particular accounting period.

○ *You are running a deficit if you spend more money than you make.*

○ *None of the companies reported a deficit during this prosperous period.*

---

de|pos|it /dɪpɒzɪt/ (deposits, deposited, depositing)

COMMERCE

VERB If you **deposit** money in a bank account, you put it there.

○ *They arranged for the money to be deposited in a bank in Andorra.*

○ *When he left the company, he deposited the checks into two unauthorized bank accounts.*

> **RELATED WORDS**
>
> The opposite of **deposit** is **withdraw**.

de|pos|it slip /dɪpɒzɪt slɪp/ (**deposit slips**)

COMMERCE

NOUN A **deposit slip** is a piece of paper listing the checks and cash being deposited in a bank account.

○ Enter all checks received on a deposit slip as well as cash receipts in a lump sum.

○ The bank teller accepted the check, attached it to the deposit slip, and forwarded it to the bank's processing depot.

▶ SYNONYM:
deposit ticket

de|pre|cia|ble /dɪpriːʃiəbəl/

TAX

ADJECTIVE If something you use for your business is **depreciable**, its loss in value over time will count toward reducing your tax.

○ The purpose of depreciation is to spread the depreciable cost of an asset over its estimated life.

○ The scheme is open to businesses with depreciable assets of less than $3 million.

▶ COLLOCATIONS:
depreciable assets
depreciable cost

> **WORD BUILDER**
> **-able** = able to be done
>
> The suffix **-able** often appears in adjectives that mean that a particular thing can be done to something: **billable**, **depreciable**, **negotiable**, **payable**, **receivable**, **taxable**.

D

de|pre|ci|a|tion /dɪpriːʃieɪʰn/

[TAX]

NOUN **Depreciation** is when the value of a tangible asset falls because of its age or how much it has been used.

○ Depreciation is deducted from gross investment to get net investment.

○ Dollar depreciation raised the cost of U.S. imports.

de|pre|ci|a|tion ex|pense /dɪpriːʃieɪʰn ɪkspɛns/
(depreciation expenses)

[FINANCIAL STATEMENTS: INCOME STATEMENT]

NOUN A **depreciation expense** is the amount deducted from gross profit to allow for a reduction in the value of something because of its age or how much it has been used.

○ When you buy and own equipment, your business may be entitled to deduct a depreciation expense.

○ The depreciation expense is the cost of using an asset and it is assigned as either a cost of production or an expense of earning the revenues of the period.

di|rect /dɪrɛkt/

[MANAGEMENT]

ADJECTIVE **Direct** costs or labor are costs or labor directly related to the production of an item.

○ Direct costs can be easily attributed to a specific item or process, and they vary according to the main activity of the business.

○ Traditionally, companies distribute their overhead between different products in the same ratio as the respective costs of direct labor in those products.

> **RELATED WORDS**
>
> Compare **direct costs** to **indirect costs** that are not directly associated with the production of goods.

dis|count|ed cash flow (ABBR DCF) /dɪskaʊntɪd kæʃ floʊ/

INVESTING

NOUN **Discounted cash flow** is a way of appraising an investment that takes into account the different values of future returns according to when they will be received.

○ *The purpose of discounted cash flow is to estimate market value, or to estimate what investors would pay for a stock or business.*

○ *Discounted cash flow is a cash flow associated with economic projects that are adjusted to allow for the timing of the cash flow and the potential interest on the funds involved.*

di|ver|si|fi|ca|tion /dɪvɜrsɪfɪkeɪʃᵊn/

INVESTING

NOUN **Diversification** is the act of investing in a variety of different industries, areas, and financial instruments, in order to reduce the risk that all the investments will drop in price at the same time.

○ *Diversification calls for spreading the portfolio among different types of assets, including not only stocks but also bonds, real estate, international investments, and cash equivalents.*

○ *Through diversification, investors can offset losses on some investments with gains on others.*

div|i|dends /dɪvɪdɛndz/

INVESTING

NOUN **Dividends** are the part of a company's profits that is paid out to the shareholders.

○ *The company's acquisitions will eventually result in higher dividends for shareholders.*

○ *The company is distributing 32 percent of its profits for 2011, but has given shareholders the option of receiving those dividends in shares, which conserves capital.*

dol|lar cost av|er|ag|ing (ABBR DCA) /dɒlər kɒst ævərədʒɪŋ/

INVESTING

NOUN **Dollar cost averaging** is the act of investing a set amount in stocks or other securities during each accounting period, so that you buy more when the price is low and less when the price is high.

○ *Thanks to dollar cost averaging, you don't have to worry whether the market is up or down.*

○ *Dollar cost averaging works best with volatile investments, and it is when prices are down that you are really planting the seeds for future profits.*

dou|ble en|try /dʌbᵊl ɛntri/

BASIC

NOUN **Double entry** is a bookkeeping system in which all transactions are entered in two places, as a debit in one account and as a credit in another.

○ *The required double entry is a debit to the long-term work in progress account to increase the value of the asset, and a credit to the profit and loss account.*

○ *The accounting books seem to have been kept by double entry, as all transactions were entered twice – to the credit of one account and to the debit of another.*

due date /du deɪt/ (due dates)

COMMERCE

NOUN The **due date** for a payment is the date by which it is to be paid.

○ *You must pay the interest within 30 days of the due date, to avert a default.*

○ *The investor group agreed to extend the due date of the existing $6 million loan from January to October.*

Ee

earn|ings /ˈɜrnɪŋz/

BASIC

NOUN **Earnings** are the amount of profit that a person or company receives after taxes have been paid.

- ○ *Average weekly earnings rose by 1.5 percent in July.*
- ○ *The company warned of lower-than-expected earnings for the fiscal year that ended June 30.*

earn|ings per share (ABBR **EPS**) /ˈɜrnɪŋz pər ʃɛər/

INVESTING

NOUN **Earnings per share** are the amount of net income from shares divided by the total number of shares outstanding.

- ○ *Shareholders will suffer about a 15 percent dilution in earnings per share.*
- ○ *For the nine months, they expect about 10 percent growth in earnings per share, indicating share earnings of about $2.64 for the period.*

E|BIT /ˈibɪt/ (short for **earnings before interest and tax**)

FINANCIAL STATEMENTS: INCOME STATEMENT

ABBREVIATION **EBIT** is the amount of profit that a person or company receives before interest and taxes have been deducted.

- ○ *Another measure of financial leverage is the extent to which interest is covered by EBIT plus depreciation.*
- ○ *After deducting the costs of goods sold and other expenses, the group had total EBIT of $1.610 million.*

E

E|BIT|DA /ˈibɪtdɑ/ (short for **earnings before interest, tax, depreciation and amortization**)

FINANCIAL STATEMENTS: INCOME STATEMENT

ABBREVIATION **EBITDA** is the amount of profit that a person or company receives before interest, taxes, depreciation, and amortization have been deducted.

○ Supporters of EBITDA as a measure argue that it is a good approximation for operating cash flow because it adds back depreciation and amortization, which are often major non-cash items.

○ The company has managed in three years to boost sales by nearly 400 percent while dramatically increasing both EBITDA and owners' compensation.

E|F|T /ˈi ɛf ti/ (short for **electronic funds transfer**)

COMMERCE

ABBREVIATION **EFT** is a transfer of funds that is carried out by electronic means, such as a computer.

○ EFT systems eliminate the paperwork of purchase orders, invoices, and checks.

○ The amount of the investment will be electronically deducted from her account by EFT.

end|ing in|ven|to|ry /ˈɛndɪŋ ɪnˈvᵊntɔri/ (**ending inventories**)

MANAGEMENT

NOUN An **ending inventory** is all of the goods, services, or materials that a business has available for use or sale at the end of an accounting period.

○ An item's inventory change equals its ending inventory value minus its beginning inventory value.

○ The ending inventory of one period automatically becomes the beginning inventory of the next period.

---

en|ti|ty /ɛntɪti/ (entities)

BASIC

NOUN An **entity** is a business organization such as a corporation or partnership.

○ The company disclosed that it intends to convert its Information Systems subsidiary into a separate public entity.

○ For shareholders, the benefits will accrue only if the company is divided into 2 separate entities.

---

en|try¹ /ɛntri/ (entries)

FINANCIAL STATEMENTS

NOUN An **entry** is the act of recording an item, such as a commercial transaction, in a journal, account, or register.

○ The charges include one count of bank fraud and two counts of making false entries on the books.

○ Accountants make the entries for the income statement at the same time as they prepare the balance sheet.

---

en|try² /ɛntri/ (entries)

FINANCIAL STATEMENTS

NOUN An **entry** is an item that is recorded, for example in a journal or account.

○ Because of the use of double-entry accounting principles, all the entries in the account must add up to zero.

○ In this bookkeeping system, each transaction is matched by an equal and opposite entry, so total debits must equal total credits.

e.|o.|m. /ˈiː oʊ ˈɛm/ (short for **end of month**)

BASIC

ABBREVIATION An **e.o.m.** payment is due to be paid on the last day of the month.

- ○ Most companies follow the practice of traditional e.o.m. billing.
- ○ The customer will receive a cash discount of 8 percent if the bill is paid within 10 days of the e.o.m.

eq|ui|ty /ˈɛkwɪti/

FINANCIAL STATEMENTS: BALANCE SHEET

NOUN **Equity** is the sum of your assets or investments once your debts have been subtracted.

- ○ To capture their equity, they must either sell or refinance.
- ○ The company is considering raising part of its future capital requirements by selling equity to the public.

eq|ui|ty ac|count /ˈɛkwɪti əˈkaʊnt/ (**equity accounts**)

FINANCIAL STATEMENTS: BALANCE SHEET

NOUN An **equity account** is an account recording ownership interests in a company.

- ○ He could not withdraw the funds from the equity account because this equity was being used to fund the working capital of the firm.
- ○ When shareholders receive a profit distribution, this payment is allocated to an equity account.

ex|pense¹ /ɪkˈspɛns/ (**expenses, expensed, expensing**)

TAX

VERB If you **expense** an item, you treat it as an expense for bookkeeping or tax purposes.

- ○ Borrowing is not the only way to shield income against tax. Investment in many intangible assets can be expensed immediately.
- ○ Research and development expenditures, including engineering costs, are expensed when incurred and amounted to $258.6 million in 2010.

ex|pense² /ɪkspɛns/ (expenses)

FINANCIAL STATEMENTS: INCOME STATEMENT

NOUN An **expense** is a cost involved in doing business.

○ All income and expenses must be itemized on the balance sheet.

○ There are some doubts among the banks whether the company has enough cash flow to cover the heavy interest expenses from the acquisition.

ex|pense ac|count¹ /ɪkspɛns əkaʊnt/ (expense accounts)

COMMERCE

NOUN An **expense account** is an arrangement that an employee has with an employer that allows the employee to spend money on things relating to their job, such as traveling or entertaining clients.

○ He put the restaurant bill on his expense account.

○ When you're traveling for business and you're on an expense account, you are more likely to do things you wouldn't normally do at home.

ex|pense ac|count² /ɪkspɛns əkaʊnt/ (expense accounts)

FINANCIAL STATEMENTS: INCOME STATEMENT

NOUN An **expense account** is an account showing the expenses of a company over a period of time.

○ Upon pre-payment of the expense, a journal entry is prepared to debit the expense account and credit cash.

○ When the company pays for merchandise, they debit their cash account and credit their expense account.

ex|pens|es /ɪkspɛnsɪz/

COMMERCE

NOUN **Expenses** are amounts of money that you spend while doing something in the course of your work, which will be paid back to you afterwards by an employer or be allowable against tax.

○ Her airfare and motel expenses were paid by the committee.

○ He received a daily allowance to cover his travel expenses, including meals, while away from home on business.

ex|traor|di|nar|y /ɪkstrɔ́rdᵊnɛri/

BASIC

ADJECTIVE If you describe something as **extraordinary**, you mean that it is very unusual or infrequent.

○ *Profit after tax and minority interests but before extraordinary items rose nearly 7 percent to $69.2 million.*

○ *The company will report net income for the year ended June 30 of 85 cents a share, including extraordinary income of 10 cents a share from an accounting change.*

▶ COLLOCATIONS:
extraordinary cost
extraordinary expenses
extraordinary income
extraordinary item

Ff

face val|ue /feɪs vælyu/

INVESTING

NOUN The **face value** of a coin, piece of paper money, or document is the amount of money that it is worth.

○ The company's bonds have fallen to 28 percent of their face value.

○ There is some possibility that the issuer of the securities may not be able to make its interest payments or pay back the face value of the securities when they mature.

fair mar|ket val|ue (ABBR **FMV**) /fɛər mɑrkɪt vælyu/

BASIC

NOUN The **fair market value** of an asset is what a willing buyer would pay a willing seller for it on the open market.

○ The board adopted a shareholder rights plan designed to assure holders fair value in the event of a proposed takeover.

○ Accounting rules require that investments are held at fair market value – the price at which they can be sold to a third party in an orderly transaction.

▶ SYNONYM:
current market value

FI|FO /faɪfoʊ/ (short for **first in, first out**)

MANAGEMENT

ABBREVIATION **FIFO** is a method of accounting which assumes that the oldest stock is sold first.

○ Using FIFO, the oldest purchase costs of goods are recognized as costs first.

○ The FIFO method assumes that goods are withdrawn from stock in the order in which they are received.

fi|nan|cial state|ments (INFORMAL **the financials**)
/faɪnænʃəl steɪtmənts/

FINANCIAL STATEMENTS

NOUN **Financial statements** are all of the reports that show how
a company is performing for a certain period.

○ The company belatedly reported a $6.2 million loss for the first nine months
of last year, but hasn't filed any financial statements since.

○ Auditors will overhaul the company's financial statements for the last
three years.

---

fi|nan|cial year /faɪnænʃəl yɪər/

BASIC

NOUN A **financial year** is any annual period at the end of which a firm's
accounts are closed.

○ The company's financial year ends June 30, 2012.

○ The company's net profits for the last financial year were just 2.72 percent
of its sales.

RELATED WORDS

The **financial year** and the **fiscal year** both mean the annual
period at the end of which a firm's accounts are closed. Compare
these with the following:

calendar year
a business year that goes from January 1 to December 31

tax year
a period of twelve months that is used by the government as
a basis for calculating taxes

---

fin|ished goods /fɪnɪʃt gʊdz/

MANAGEMENT

NOUN **Finished goods** are goods that have completed the
manufacturing process, but have not yet been sold.

○ Countries that mainly export raw materials are poorer, while countries that
convert them into finished goods are richer.

○*Although the cost of imports such as oil and raw materials has soared, the price of finished goods has remained stable and profit rates have not declined much.*

---

fis|cal year (ABBR **FY**) /fɪskəl yɪər/

BASIC

NOUN A **fiscal year** is a period of twelve months, used by organizations in order to calculate their budgets, profits, and losses, at the end of which a firm's accounts are closed.

○*The company is finalizing the budget for the coming fiscal year.*

○*The company's performance in the current fiscal year has been poor.*

---

fixed as|sets /fɪkst æsɛts/

FINANCIAL STATEMENTS: BALANCE SHEET

NOUN **Fixed assets** are a company's permanent assets, such as buildings, equipment, and technology.

○*There has been a drop in spending on fixed assets such as software.*

○*Assets in a company's account include fixed assets like land, plants, and machinery, as well as investments and current assets like finished goods and sundry debtors.*

---

fixed charge /fɪkst tʃɑrdʒ/ (**fixed charges**)

MANAGEMENT

NOUN A **fixed charge** is an expense that is paid regularly, such as rent.

○*The company's earnings were insufficient to cover its fixed charges.*

○*Fixed charges include such obligations as interest on bonds and notes, lease obligations, and any other recurring financial commitments.*

---

fixed costs /fɪkst kɔsts/

MANAGEMENT

NOUN **Fixed costs** are costs that do not vary depending on how much of a product is made.

○*Most companies have high fixed costs, and only once those costs are covered, profits can surge.*

F

○ *Building an infrastructure for new brands or markets means adding to fixed costs no matter what the volume of sales achieved.*

F|O|B des|ti|na|tion /ɛf oʊ biː dɛstɪneɪʃᵊn/ (short for **free on board destination**)

COMMERCE

PHRASE **FOB destination** is a shipping term indicating that ownership of goods passes at delivery to their destination, and the seller has total responsibility until then.

○ *If the terms of a sale are FOB destination, delivery generally is not considered to have occurred until a product is delivered to the customer's delivery site.*

○ *If goods are shipped FOB destination point, they remain the legal property of the seller until they reach their destination.*

F|O|B ship|ping point /ɛf oʊ biː ʃɪpɪŋ pɔɪnt/ (short for **free on board shipping point**)

COMMERCE

PHRASE **FOB shipping point** is a shipping term indicating that ownership of goods passes when they are transferred to the carrier.

○ *When the terms of shipment are FOB shipping point, the buyer incurs transportation costs.*

○ *If the buyer is responsible for paying the freight cost, the shipping terms are called FOB shipping point.*

---

foot /fʊt/ (**foots, footed, footing**)

FINANCIAL STATEMENTS

VERB If you **foot** a column in an account, you add up the numbers in the column to get the total.

○ *Balances are arrived at by footing the debit and credit columns of each account and calculating the difference between the two columns.*

○ *Once the adjustments have been recorded in the adjustments column, the accountant will foot the debit and credit adjustments column.*

foot|ing /ˈfʊtɪŋ/ (footings)

FINANCIAL STATEMENTS

NOUN A **footing** is a notation at the bottom of a column of figures showing the total.

○ The debit column footing is $11,900, and that of the credit column $1875, and you subtract one from the other to determine the balance of the account.

○ The footing serves as the balance for accounts with entries on only one side of the account.

foot|notes /ˈfʊtnoʊts/

FINANCIAL STATEMENTS

NOUN **Footnotes** are notes which provide additional detail and explanation, particularly for financial statements.

○ The footnotes provide additional information about the basic figures included in the financial statements.

○ Registrants should disclose in the footnotes to the financial statements the amounts of the unearned revenue.

free cash flow /fri kæʃ floʊ/ (free cash flows)

MANAGEMENT

COUNT/NONCOUNT NOUN **Free cash flow** is revenue of a business that is available to spend.

○ Cash not retained and reinvested in the business is often known as free cash flow.

○ It is our goal to grow sales at an average annual rate of 10 to 12 percent with operating margins of at least 15 percent and to generate approximately $100 million in free cash flow.

freight-in /freɪt ɪn/

COMMERCE

NOUN **Freight-in** is the cost of having goods or materials delivered to a business for manufacture or resale.

○ When the buyer pays for the cost of freight, the buyer records the cost as freight-in.

○ *The freight-in account is used only to record the incoming transportation charges on merchandise intended for resale.*

---

freight-out /freɪt aʊt/

COMMERCE

NOUN **Freight-out** is the cost of delivering finished goods to a customer.

○ *The cost of freight charges paid to ship goods sold to customers is called freight-out, and it is paid by the seller, not by the purchaser.*

○ *When the seller pays the transportation charge, it is called delivery expense, or freight-out.*

---

func|tion|al cur|ren|cy /fʌŋkʃənəl kɜrənsi/ (functional currencies)

FINANCIAL STATEMENTS

NOUN **Functional currency** is the main currency used by a business.

○ *A British subsidiary of a US parent firm will declare that the pound is its functional currency, into which any foreign-currency income is translated.*

○ *If an item is denominated in the functional currency of the foreign operation, an exchange difference arises.*

---

funds /fʌndz/

BASIC

NOUN **Funds** are money that is readily available.

○ *The government should not be using public funds to pay for these services.*

○ *If the investor loans are not provided and adequate funds from other sources are not available by April 30, the company will be required to terminate its operations.*

Gg

GAAP /gæp/ (short for **Generally Accepted Accounting Principles**)

FINANCIAL STATEMENTS

ABBREVIATION In the US, **GAAP** are rules to which financial statements of publicly traded companies must conform.

○ Many insurance companies, particularly mutuals, do not report their data in GAAP terms.

○ The company needs to refinance a $2.65 billion loan on which it is now in default because its accounts no longer comply with GAAP standards.

---

gain on sale /ɡeɪn ɒn seɪl/ (**gains on sale**)

FINANCIAL STATEMENTS: INCOME STATEMENT

NOUN A **gain on sale** is the amount of money that is made by a company when selling a non-inventory asset for more than its value.

○ Other income and expense consists primarily of interest expense, interest income, and gain on sale of stock of a third party.

○ At the end of the accounting period, any gain on sale of securities must be included on the income statement.

---

gain on trans|la|tion /ɡeɪn ɒn trænzleɪʃən/ (**gains on translation**)

FINANCIAL STATEMENTS: INCOME STATEMENT

NOUN A **gain on translation** is the amount of money that is made by a company by converting another currency used in a transaction into the functional currency of the company.

○ A gain on translation is recorded for a loan payable denominated in a foreign currency when the dollar has increased in value compared to the foreign currency.

○ *Companies using the current rate method generally show a gain on translation when the US dollar weakens and a loss when the US dollar strengthens.*

---

gains /geɪnz/

BASIC

NOUN **Gains** are profits that are made by selling non-inventory assets.

○ *The company posted big earnings gains for the quarter, as expected.*

○ *The company made significant gains in the second quarter of 2009 when it sold patents that were not currently used in the company's products or development projects.*

---

gen|er|al jour|nal /dʒɛnərəl dʒɜːrnᵊl/ (**general journals**)

FINANCIAL STATEMENTS

NOUN A **general journal** is a journal recording all of the transactions of a business.

○ *As soon as a business transaction takes place, it is recorded in the general journal.*

○ *Transactions are recorded in either the general journal or a special journal, but not in both.*

---

gen|er|al ledg|er (ABBR **GL**) /dʒɛnərəl lɛdʒər/ (**general ledgers**)

FINANCIAL STATEMENTS

NOUN A **general ledger** is the final record of all of the accounts posted from the journals of a business, which is used to prepare financial statements.

○ *Two senior controllers produced a general ledger showing financial results for each quarter and for year end.*

○ *The controller created a numerical range of accounts in the general ledger in which he recorded the transferred amounts.*

gen|er|al part|ner|ship /dʒɛnərəl pɑrtnərʃɪp/ (general partnerships)

`BASIC`

NOUN A **general partnership** is a form of partnership in which the partners are all liable for the activities of the partnership.

○ *In a general partnership, active owners, called general partners, have unlimited liability for all business debts.*

○ *An investment general partnership is functionally a vehicle in which profits and losses are passed through to general partners.*

goods /gʊdz/

`COMMERCE`

NOUN **Goods** are things that are made to be sold.

○ *Money can be exchanged for goods or services.*

○ *Britain's main trading partners have been trapped in low or no growth, unable to buy more goods and services.*

good|will /gʊdwɪl/

`FINANCIAL STATEMENTS: BALANCE SHEET`

NOUN **Goodwill** is an intangible asset that is taken into account when the value of an enterprise is calculated, reflecting the company's reputation and its relationship with its customers.

○ *A major factor in the third-quarter loss was the write-down of $143.6 million of goodwill.*

○ *Usually, the largest intangible asset that appears on a company's balance sheet is goodwill, which is the value of all favorable attributes that relate to a business enterprise.*

gross¹ /groʊs/

`BASIC`

ADJECTIVE **Gross** refers to the total amount of something, especially money, before anything has been taken away.

○ *This is a fixed-rate account guaranteeing 10.4 percent gross interest or 7.8 percent net.*

○ *Annual gross revenue from the facility is expected to be about $5 million.*

▶ **COLLOCATIONS:**
gross amount
gross revenue
gross sales
gross total

RELATED WORDS

The opposite of **gross** is **net**. The net amount of something is the amount that remains after subtracting taxes, expenses, losses, and costs.

---

gross² /grəʊs/ (grosses, grossed, grossing)

FINANCIAL STATEMENTS: INCOME STATEMENT

VERB If a person or a company **grosses** a particular amount of money, they earn it as total revenue, before deductions such as expenses and tax.

○ *The popular brand grossed $65 million in sales last year.*

○ *By her third year, she was grossing $6 million, thanks to a fortuitous contract with the superstore.*

---

gross prof|it (INFORMAL the gross) /grəʊs prɒfɪt/ (gross profits)

FINANCIAL STATEMENTS: INCOME STATEMENT

NOUN A company's **gross profit** is the difference between its total income from sales and its total production costs.

○ *Gross profit is the figure obtained on the profit and loss account when the cost of goods sold is deducted from the sales revenue of a business.*

○ *A typical luxury car makes a gross profit of around 15–20 percent of its sales price, and small cars barely break even.*

▶ **SYNONYM:**
gross margin

gross prof|it mar|gin /ɡrəʊs prɒfɪt mɑːdʒɪn/ (**gross profit margins**)

INVESTING

NOUN A **gross profit margin** is a measure of the profitability of a company, that is calculated by dividing gross profit by net sales.

○ Trade publications claim his gross profit margins approach 10 percent, well above the industry norm.

○ A reasonable approximation to cost must be given, usually by deducting a gross profit margin from the full selling price.

▶ **SYNONYMS:**
  gross margin percentage
  gross margin ratio
  gross profit percentage

gross up /ɡrəʊs ʌp/ (**grosses up, grossed up, grossing up**)

BASIC

VERB If you **gross up** net income or wages, you increase them to their value before tax or deductions.

○ The tax breaks mean that every dollar that you pay into your pension will be grossed up to $1.28.

○ Your investment benefits from being grossed up by basic rate tax relief.

Hh

hard cop|y /hɑrd kɒpi/ (hard copies)

BASIC

NOUN A **hard copy** is a paper document as opposed to an electronic one.

- ○ Can you mail me a hard copy of the document as well as sending it
  electronically?
- ○ The data from companies will be available in both hard copy form and on
  the Internet.

hedge /hɛdʒ/ (hedges, hedged, hedging)

INVESTING

VERB If you **hedge**, you reduce risk when conducting a transaction by
doing an opposite transaction.

- ○ Investors were plowing their funds into oil and other commodities to hedge
  against inflation.
- ○ Private companies owe more than half of the country's foreign debt, much of
  it consisting of loans which were not hedged against currency risks.

his|tor|i|cal cost /hɪstɒrɪkəl kɔst/ (historical costs)

FINANCIAL STATEMENTS

NOUN The **historical cost** of an asset is its original cost when it was first
acquired by a company.

- ○ Using the historical cost of the asset, the charge is based on the prices
  prevailing when the asset was purchased.
- ○ The value of goods held in inventory is stated at historical cost, and even if
  prices change, the objective price is that which the business paid historically.

hy|brid ba|sis /ˈhaɪbrɪd ˈbeɪsɪs/

FINANCIAL STATEMENTS

NOUN A **hybrid basis** is a system of accounting that combines some of the features of cost basis with some of the features of accrual basis.

○ When a business registers for Goods and Services Tax, it has to choose whether to account for the tax on a cash, accrual, or hybrid basis.

○ Identifiable net assets of the subsidiary would be valued on a hybrid basis, rather than at full current fair values.

h

Ii

im|pair|ment /ɪmpɛərmənt/

FINANCIAL STATEMENTS

NOUN **Impairment** is the situation when the current value of an asset is less than the historical cost.

○ Banks were partly responsible for the impairment of their asset portfolios because of their imprudent lending and investment policies.

○ Asset impairment happens when the carrying amount of an asset is greater than the amount recoverable either through using or selling an asset.

in|come /ɪnkʌm/

BASIC

NOUN **Income** is the money that a person or company earns or receives, as opposed to the money that they have to spend or pay out.

○ They have the expertise of running low-cost operations in markets where consumers have very low incomes.

○ The company reported that net income for the fiscal first quarter more than doubled.

in|come ac|count /ɪnkʌm əkaʊnt/ (income accounts)

FINANCIAL STATEMENTS: INCOME STATEMENT

NOUN An **income account** is an account that records income or revenue.

○ If you want to record income, you credit the income account.

○ Each major source of income needs a separate income account.

in|come state|ment /ɪnkʌm steɪtmənt/ (**income statements**)

FINANCIAL STATEMENTS: INCOME STATEMENT

NOUN An **income statement** is a financial statement showing the revenues and expenses of a company over a period of time.

○ If the firm has a deficit in its income statement, it must borrow, raise more equity, or divest itself of assets purchased in the past.

○ Members of the audit committee must be able to read and understand fundamental financial statements, including a company's balance sheet, income statement, and cash flow statement.

▶ **SYNONYMS:**
profit and loss statement
statement of income and expenses

in|come tax /ɪnkʌm tæks/

TAX

NOUN **Income tax** is a part of your income that you have to pay regularly to the government.

○ You pay income tax every month on your earnings.

○ You pay income tax on all your earnings, not just your salary.

in|de|pend|ent con|trac|tor /ɪndɪpɛndənt kɒntræktər/ (**independent contractors**)

BASIC

NOUN An **independent contractor** is a person who is in business for themselves, and is hired to perform a task or service for a company.

○ Current law makes it difficult for business owners to determine whether a worker is an independent contractor or an employee.

○ She likes the benefits of being an independent contractor – the autonomy, higher salary, and ability to experience a wide variety of companies.

in|di|rect /ɪndaɪrɛkt/

MANAGEMENT

ADJECTIVE A company's **indirect** costs are costs that are not directly associated with the production of goods.

○ *The direct and indirect costs associated with absenteeism alone are almost $350,000 per year.*

○ *Absorption costing is a technique by which the overhead and indirect costs associated with a product, contract, or service are allocated to that unit.*

WORD BUILDER
in- = not

The prefix **in-** is often added to adjectives to make their opposites: **indirect**, **insolvent**, **intangible**.

---

in|i|tial pub|lic of|fer|ing (ABBR **IPO**) /ɪnɪʃ°l pʌblɪk ɔfərɪŋ/
(initial public offerings)

INVESTING

NOUN An **initial public offering** is the first offering of stock when a company goes public. The abbreviation can also informally be used as a verb: "to IPO."

○ *The company began an initial public offering of 1.5 million common shares at $9 each, or a total of $13.5 million.*

○ *In an initial public offering, underwriters priced 2.5 million shares at $14 each.*

---

in|sol|vent /ɪnsɒlv°nt/
BASIC

ADJECTIVE If you are **insolvent**, you do not have enough money to pay your debts.

○ *The bank was declared insolvent and closed in December.*

○ *He was required to declare himself an insolvent debtor, to detail all of his debts, and to hold goods valued at no more than $20.*

---

in|stall|ment sales /ɪnstɔlmənt seɪlz/
COMMERCE

NOUN **Installment sales** are sales where fixed payments will be made regularly over a particular period of time.

○ *Taxes on installment sales are deferred until all payments are collected.*

○ *In installment sales, the purchaser agrees to pay for the purchase in a series of periodic payments.*

in|sur|ance /ɪnʃʊərəns/

BASIC

NOUN **Insurance** is an arrangement in which you regularly pay money to a company, and they pay you if something bad happens to you or your property.

○ *The house had to be demolished, and the insurance company promptly paid us the policy limit.*

○ *The provision allows an investor to buy insurance against a company defaulting on its debt payments.*

in|tan|gi|ble as|sets /ɪntændʒɪbəl æsɛts/

FINANCIAL STATEMENTS

NOUN **Intangible assets** are assets which are not physical, such as trademarks, customer lists, and goodwill.

○ *Assets such as patents, trademarks, or goodwill are known as intangible assets in contrast to the physical ones such as plant and machinery.*

○ *Accountants are struggling to find a way to measure such intangible assets as a company's research and development, the value of its brands, and even its general reputation.*

in|tel|lec|tu|al prop|er|ty (ABBR **IP**) /ɪntɪlɛktʃuəl prɒpərti/

BASIC

NOUN **Intellectual property** is something such as an invention or a copyright that is officially owned by someone.

○ *If there is to be innovation, the firm insists, intellectual property must be protected.*

○ *Music and films are defined as intellectual property, and owned by named individuals or companies.*

in|ter|est /ɪntrɪst/

BASIC

NOUN **Interest** is the extra money that you pay if you have borrowed money, or the extra money that you receive if you have money in some types of bank account.

○ The home buyer puts up the other half of the closing costs and fee, and then pays interest at 12 percent a year to the investor.

○ Investors want to lend because lenders would typically receive the 10–15 percent interest on the loan.

---

in|ter|est rate /ɪntrɪst reɪt/ (interest rates)
BASIC

NOUN The **interest rate** is the amount of interest that must be paid on a loan or investment, expressed as a percentage of the amount that is borrowed or gained as profit.

○ The Federal Reserve lowered interest rates by half a point.

○ Usually, short-term interest rates are lower than long-term rates, because investors want higher rates the longer they lend their money.

---

in|ter|nal rate of re|turn (ABBR IRR) /ɪntɜːnᵊl reɪt əv rɪtɜːn/
MANAGEMENT

NOUN The **internal rate of return** is the interest rate at which a project would break even.

○ Use the internal rate of return to assess the acceptability of independent projects.

○ The internal rate of return is defined as the rate of discount at which a project would have zero net present value.

---

in|ven|to|ry¹ /ɪnvᵊntɔri/ (inventories)
MANAGEMENT

COUNT/NONCOUNT NOUN The **inventory** of a business is the amount or value of its raw materials, work in progress, and finished goods.

○ Second-quarter growth slowed because distributors had too much inventory.

○ Piled-up inventories block working capital, and add to its costs.

▶ **SYNONYM:**
stock

in|ven|to|ry² /ɪnvᵊntɔri/ (**inventories, inventoried, inventorying**)

MANAGEMENT

VERB If you **inventory** items in the inventory of a business, you count them.

○ *A product cost can be inventoried and can remain an asset as part of the materials, work in process, or finished goods inventory.*

○ *Each product must be tracked, shelved, and inventoried.*

in|ven|to|ry turn|o|ver /ɪnvᵊntɔri tɜrnoʊvər/

MANAGEMENT

NOUN **Inventory turnover** is a measure of the efficiency of a company, that is calculated by dividing the cost of goods sold by average inventory.

○ *A high inventory turnover is often regarded as a sign of efficiency.*

○ *The inventory turnover ratio indicates the number of times inventory is sold during the year.*

in|vest|ment /ɪnvɛstmənt/ (**investments**)

INVESTING

COUNT/NONCOUNT NOUN **Investment** is the activity of investing money. An **investment** is an amount of money that you invest, or the thing that you invest it in.

○ *He has made a $1 million investment in the company.*

○ *The government is very open to foreign investment in the airline.*

in|voice¹ /ɪnvɔɪs/ (**invoices**)

COMMERCE

NOUN An **invoice** is a document issued by a seller to a buyer that lists the goods or services that have been supplied and says how much money the buyer owes for them.

○ *The invoice will show the goods ordered and purchased, their quantity, their unit and total price, and any VAT being charged on the purchase.*

○ *Once the sales and marketing department allots the car, the finance department prints out the invoice for the dealer, and the car is delivered.*

---

in|voice² /ɪnvɔɪs/ (**invoices, invoiced, invoicing**)

COMMERCE

VERB If you **invoice** a customer, you send or give them a bill for goods or services that you have provided them with.

○ *The agency invoices the client who then pays.*

○ *In industry, it is normal practice to invoice the customer and for the customer to pay the bill in due course.*

---

in|voice³ /ɪnvɔɪs/ (**invoices, invoiced, invoicing**)

COMMERCE

VERB If you **invoice** goods that have been sold, you list them on an invoice.

○ *The bulk of cross-border sales are invoiced and settled in dollars.*

○ *Sales are recognized in the period in which they are invoiced.*

---

i|tem /aɪtəm/ (**items**)

FINANCIAL STATEMENTS / COMMERCE

NOUN An **item** is an entry in an account.

○ *The auditors do not verify every item in the company's books and instead they take samples.*

○ *The next three items in the current account are the net payments or receipts that arise from investment income.*

Jj

jour|nal /dʒɜːnᵊl/ (journals)

FINANCIAL STATEMENTS

NOUN A **journal** is a book in which transactions are recorded before they are entered into a ledger.

○ *The journal shows all purchases, sales, receipts, and deliveries of securities, and all other debits and credits.*

○ *Transactions are periodically posted from the journal to ledger accounts.*

▶ **SYNONYMS:**
book of account
book of original entry
daybook

> **RELATED WORDS**
>
> A **ledger** is a book in which a company or organization writes down the amounts of money that it spends and receives, and a **cash book** is a book in which all cash or check receipts and expenditures are recorded.

jour|nal en|try (ABBR **JE**) /dʒɜːnᵊl ɛntri/ (journal entries)

FINANCIAL STATEMENTS

NOUN A **journal entry** is an entry made directly into the general journal.

○ *A journal entry uses a standardized format to indicate the accounts and amounts affected by each transaction.*

○ *Each journal entry will have at least one debit and one credit as a part of the entry.*

Kk

---

keep the books /kɪp ðə bʊks/

PHRASE If you **keep the books**, you keep written records of the finances of a business or other enterprise.

- ○ *The accounts of public institutions are audited by qualified persons who are independent of those who keep the books.*
- ○ *The accountants who keep the books for a company should be different from those who are auditing the company's books.*

K

Ll

lease¹ /liːs/ (leases, leased, leasing)

COMMERCE

VERB If you **lease** an asset such as a car or building or **lease** it **from** someone, you pay them, and they allow you to use it.

○ *The company is being squeezed by competitors as well as customer preferences for leasing rather than buying systems.*

○ *The threat of further industrial action has involved the company in commitments to lease planes from other airlines.*

lease² /liːs/ (leases)

COMMERCE

NOUN A **lease** is a legal agreement that allows someone to pay money so that they can use an asset such as a car or building for a particular period of time.

○ *The lease on the building will be up in May.*

○ *They signed a lease for 426,000 square feet of office space.*

lease-back /liːs bæk/ (lease-backs)

COMMERCE

NOUN A **lease-back** is an agreement in which one person or company sells property to another, who then leases the property back to the seller.

○ *When the lessor acquires the asset from the user and then leases it back to them, it is known as a sale and lease-back.*

○ *The buyers will receive lease-back guarantees of 9 percent of the apartment price annually for two years.*

lease with op|tion to buy /lis wɪð ɒpʃᵊn tə baɪ/
(leases with option to buy)

COMMERCE

NOUN A **lease with option to buy** is a lease that states that the person leasing the property has the right to purchase it at the end of the lease period.

○ *If you're ready to buy a house, but your credit or savings aren't quite ready yet, a lease with option to buy may help you move in.*

○ *The agreement is a lease with option to buy, so you can rent it for $1850 a month, and $400 of the rent goes toward the purchase price of your option.*

ledg|er /lɛdʒər/ (ledgers)

FINANCIAL STATEMENTS

NOUN A **ledger** is a book in which a company or organization writes down the amounts of money that it spends and receives.

○ *The only evidence that the customer owes you money is the entry in your ledger and a receipt signed by the customer.*

○ *We maintain a ledger of money and goods coming in and going out.*

les|see /lɛsi/ (lessees)

COMMERCE

NOUN A **lessee** is a person who is paying to lease an asset such as a car or building.

○ *The lessee must make a series of fixed payments and, if they fail to do so, the lessor can repossess the asset.*

○ *In a net lease, the lessee agrees to maintain the asset, insure it, and pay any property taxes.*

WORD BUILDER

-ee = person something is done to

The suffix **-ee** is sometimes used to change a verb into a noun meaning "the person the thing is done to:" **lessee**, **payee**.

---

les|sor /lɛsɔr/ (**lessors**)

COMMERCE

NOUN A **lessor** is the owner of an asset such as a car or building, who is renting it out to the lessee.

○ Under a full-service or rental lease, the lessor promises to maintain and insure the equipment and to pay any property taxes due on it.

○ Leases come in many forms, but in all cases the lessee promises to make a series of payments to the lessor.

let|ter of cred|it /lɛtər əv krɛdɪt/ (**letters of credit**)

COMMERCE

NOUN A **letter of credit** is a letter written by a bank authorizing another bank to pay someone a sum of money.

○ If a seller agrees to be paid by a letter of credit, then you need a reliable bank to handle the transaction.

○ The project is being backed by a letter of credit from Lasalle Bank.

lev|er|age /lɛvərɪdʒ/

INVESTING

NOUN **Leverage** is the amount of borrowed money that a company uses to run its business.

○ Converting either of those two securities into debt would only further raise the debt leverage of the buy-out.

○ Financial leverage is usually measured by the ratio of long-term debt to total long-term capital.

li|a|bil|i|ties /laɪəbɪlɪtiz/ (**liability**)

FINANCIAL STATEMENTS: BALANCE SHEET

NOUN A company's **liabilities** are the sums of money which it owes, that are entered as claims on the assets shown on the balance sheet.

○ The company had assets of $138 million, and liabilities of $120.5 million.

○ The protection regulation shields parent corporations from the liabilities of their subsidiaries.

li|a|bil|i|ty ac|count /laɪəbɪlɪti əkaʊnt/ **(liability accounts)**

FINANCIAL STATEMENTS: BALANCE SHEET

NOUN A **liability account** is an account recording a company's liabilities.

○ *The amount of the fee representing estimated refunds should be credited to a monetary liability account.*

○ *The original entry to record unearned revenue involves a debit to Cash and a credit to a liability account.*

li|cense /laɪsᵊns/ **(licenses)**

BASIC

NOUN A **license** is an official document that gives you permission to do, use, or own something.

○ *The company manufactures Marlboro under license from Philip Morris.*

○ *If a licensed product or technology is physically delivered to the customer, but the license term has not yet begun, revenue should not be recognized prior to inception of the license term.*

li|censed /laɪsᵊnst/

BASIC

ADJECTIVE If something that you use or own is **licensed**, or you are **licensed** to do something, you have official permission to do, use, or own something.

○ *A state agency sets the rates, and licensed insurers in the state must use these rates.*

○ *In Germany, Denmark, and Holland, garlic is a licensed medicine for cholesterol reduction.*

LI|FO /laɪfoʊ/ (short for **last in, first out**)

MANAGEMENT

ABBREVIATION **LIFO** is a method of valuing inventory which assumes that the newest stock is sold first.

○ *LIFO is not generally accepted as a suitable method of stock valuation because it does not reflect normal practice in which oldest stock is used first.*

○ Using LIFO, the last costs of goods are recognized as costs first, leaving the oldest costs in the value of inventory.

---

lim|it|ed part|ner|ship /lɪmɪtɪd pɑrtnərʃɪp/ (**limited partnerships**)

BASIC

NOUN A **limited partnership** is a form of partnership in which some of the partners contribute only financially and are liable only to the extent of the amount of money that they have invested.

○ In a limited partnership structure, limited partners are shielded to the extent of their investment.

○ Usually, the limited partnership has a general partner who has unlimited liability but allows other partners to limit their potential loss.

---

liq|uid as|sets /lɪkwɪd æsɛts/

BASIC

NOUN **Liquid assets** are assets that can be easily converted into cash.

○ A company's most liquid assets are its holdings of cash and marketable securities.

○ Broker-dealers must have at all times enough liquid assets to promptly satisfy the claims of customers if the broker-dealer goes out of business.

▶ **SYNONYM:**
quick assets

---

li|quid|i|ty /lɪkwɪdɪti/

BASIC

NOUN A company's **liquidity** is its ability to turn its assets into cash.

○ One way to ensure liquidity is to maintain large cash balances or arrange necessary borrowing facilities but neither approach results in optimal profitability.

○ The company had to ensure cash flows and liquidity, and also had to generate sufficient profits at the end of the day to ensure dividends for shareholders.

list price /lɪst praɪs/ (**list prices**)

COMMERCE

NOUN The **list price** is the price that the manufacturer of an item suggests that a store should charge for it.

○ *This is a small car with a list price of $18,000.*

○ *The new printers would have a list price between $1,700 and $2,000*

▶ SYNONYM:
  retail price

L|L|C /ɛl ɛl siː/ (short for **limited liability company**)

BASIC

ABBREVIATION An **LLC** is a form of company that limits the amount of liability undertaken by the company's shareholders.

○ *The organization will be incorporated as an LLC corporation which will shield the owner and the three outside investors from issues of personal liability and double taxation.*

○ *An advantage of an LLC is that none of the owners are personally liable for its debts.*

loan /loʊn/ (**loans**)

BASIC

NOUN A **loan** is an amount of money that you borrow.

○ *The company had taken out a bank loan to finance the purchase.*

○ *The president wants to make it easier for small businesses to get bank loans.*

TALKING ABOUT LOANS

You **take out** a loan or **secure** a loan. When you pay the money back, you **repay** it.

When someone organizes a loan, they **arrange** it or **fix** it.

If someone **guarantees** a loan, they agree to pay back the money if the person who gets the loan does not.

With a **fixed-rate** loan, the amount of interest you pay stays the same, and with an **interest-free** loan, you do not pay any interest.

---

lock|box /lɒkbɒks/ (lockboxes)

COMMERCE

NOUN A **lockbox** is a bank account set up to receive payments from customers.

○ A company can use a lockbox service, whereby the bank receives and processes checks on its behalf.

○ A lockbox is an arrangement with a bank under which payments are mailed to a strategically located post office box that is serviced by the bank.

long-term /lɔŋ tɜrm/

BASIC

ADJECTIVE Something that is **long-term** has continued for more than a year or will continue for more than a year.

○ Short-term interest rates are lower than long-term rates, because investors want higher rates the longer they lend their money.

○ More than 95 percent of the money raised by the company is long-term debt.

long-term li|a|bil|i|ties /lɔŋ tɜrm laɪəbɪlɪtiz/

FINANCIAL STATEMENTS: BALANCE SHEET

NOUN **Long-term liabilities** are debts that a company does not have to pay back for a year or more.

○ On the right-hand side of the balance sheet, we find total long-term liabilities of $694 billion.

○ Bonds and leases that will not be repaid for many years are shown as long-term liabilities.

loss /lɔs/ (losses)

FINANCIAL STATEMENTS: INCOME STATEMENT

NOUN If a business reports a **loss**, it earns less money than it spends.

○ The company suffered a loss of $270 million.

○ The company expects to report a loss for its fiscal-fourth quarter ended June 30 compared with net income of $1.4 million, or 16 cents a share, a year earlier.

> **TALKING ABOUT LOSSES**
>
> If a company makes losses, it **incurs** or **accumulates** them.
>
> When a company formally announces its losses, it **posts**, **reports**, or **records** them.
>
> If a company **offsets** its losses, it uses something else to make them smaller.

---

loss|es /lɒsɪz/

BASIC

NOUN **Losses** are money that is lost by selling non-inventory assets.

○ The trust funds often took substantial losses when the securities were sold later.

○ They have pledged about $250 million to restore the net worth of some subsidiary banks and cover losses from problem assets.

---

loss on sale /lɒs ɒn seɪl/ (**losses on sale**)

FINANCIAL STATEMENTS

NOUN A **loss on sale** is the amount of money that is lost by a company when selling a non-inventory asset for more than its value.

○ The current cost net book value is $7200, so if the asset is being sold for $5000, there is a resulting loss on sale of $2200.

○ The sale price of the car is below its fair value by Rs 15.000, but the loss on sale is compensated due to the rental for the car being lower than the normal rental by Rs 10000 per year.

---

loss on trans|la|tion /lɒs ɒn trænzleɪʃ°n/ (**losses on translation**)

FINANCIAL STATEMENTS

NOUN A **loss on translation** is the amount of money that is lost by a company by converting another currency used in a transaction into the functional currency of the company.

○ If the exchange rate increases beyond this rate on the date of withdrawal, the additional loss on translation of liability will be debited to the profit and loss account.

○ *When an entity translates their foreign currency into the functional currency of their enterprise, any resulting loss on translation should be recognized in an entity's profit and loss account.*

---

low|er of cost or mar|ket /ˈloʊər əv kɔst ər ˈmɑrkɪt/

FINANCIAL STATEMENTS

PHRASE **Lower of cost or market** is a method of valuing assets where the asset is valued at either the historical cost or the fair market value, whichever is lower.

○ *When the value of the inventory has declined below its cost, a firm may choose the lower of cost or market method.*

○ *If the cost of replacing inventory is lower than its recorded purchase cost, the lower-of-cost-or-market method is used to value the inventory.*

Mm

man|u|fac|tur|ing /mænyəfæktʃərɪŋ/

BASIC

NOUN **Manufacturing** is the business of making things in factories.

○ *Manufacturing, especially of steel and cars, accounts for over a quarter of the state's output.*

○ *A manufacturing company converts raw materials into finished goods.*

mar|gin¹ /mɑrdʒɪn/ (margins)

COMMERCE

NOUN A **margin** is the difference between the selling price and the cost of an item.

○ *Because the soft-drink bottler actually stocks the supermarket's shelves, store operators save on labor costs and generate very lucrative margins on soda sales.*

○ *There is no reason why we cannot improve our margins by focusing on our operational efficiencies.*

> **TALKING ABOUT MARGINS**
>
> Something that makes a margin smaller **reduces**, **erodes**, or **squeezes** it. Small margins are described as **narrow**, **slim**, or **tight**.
>
> Something that makes a margin bigger **improves** it. Large margins are described as **high** or **healthy**.

mar|gin² /mɑrdʒɪn/ (margins)

INVESTING

NOUN If you buy stocks **on the margin**, you borrow money in order to buy them, in the hope that they will increase in value before you have to pay the loan back.

○ *The government expanded the scope of permissible capital market activities, such as allowing finance companies to fund equity purchases on the margin.*

○ *People are borrowing on credit cards to gamble on the margin, so that they quickly climb into serious debt to try to recoup losses.*

---

mark down /mɑrk daʊn/ (marks down, marked down, marking down)

COMMERCE

VERB If you **mark down** something that you are selling, you reduce the selling price.

○ *Rather than marking down menu prices, the chain would offer coupons giving patrons a discount on certain items.*

○ *If a product is not selling, its price is marked down within a specified period.*

▶ **COLLOCATIONS:**
mark down a price
mark down a product

---

mar|ket /mɑrkɪt/ (markets)

INVESTING

NOUN The **market** for a particular product is the people who want to buy it.

○ *The two big companies control 72 percent of the market.*

○ *The company sees strong demand for its products, and believes the market for computer workstations remains healthy.*

TALKING ABOUT MARKETS

If a company starts selling a particular thing, it **enters** that market. If it makes products that people want to buy, it **taps** a particular market.

If a company sells more than other companies in a particular market, it **dominates** that market, or **corners** the market.

If a company sells so much of a product that it is not worth another company trying to sell it, it **floods** or **saturates** the market.

> A strong market can be described as **booming** or **buoyant**.
> A market that is not stable is **volatile** or **jittery**, and a market in
> which sales are slow is **sluggish**.

mark-to-mar|ket /mɑrk tə mɑrkɪt/

FINANCIAL STATEMENTS

PHRASE **Mark-to-market** is the process of adjusting the value of an
asset on the balance sheet to reflect the current market price, instead
of the historical cost.

○ Mark-to-market accounting meant that banks were valuing illiquid assets at
prices which reflected a lack of buyers as much as underlying credit quality.

○ There is fierce criticism against mark-to-market accounting, which forces
banks to value assets at the estimated price they would fetch if sold now,
rather than at historical cost.

mark-up /mɑrk ʌp/ (mark-ups)

COMMERCE

NOUN A **mark-up** is a percentage that is added to the cost of a product,
in order to cover costs and provide profit.

○ The firm imports cement and sells it at a 10 percent mark-up.

○ The producer will allow the retailer to put on a mark-up to obtain profit, but
the producers will not incur the distribution costs to the consumer.

ma|te|ri|al /mətɪəriəl/

BASIC

ADJECTIVE A **material** amount of something is an amount that would
make a difference, especially in an accounting calculation.

○ An audit seeks to provide only reasonable assurance that the statements are
free from material error.

○ The risk of material misstatement of the financial statements is generally
greater when account balances and classes of transactions include
accounting estimates rather than factual data.

▶ COLLOCATION:
material error

mer|chan|dise /mɜrtʃəndaɪz/

COMMERCE

NOUN **Merchandise** is products that are bought, sold, or traded.

○ Several stores have reported running out of merchandise.

○ Only a small percentage of merchandise is returned because of defects.

mer|chant ac|count /mɜrtʃənt əkaʊnt/ (**merchant accounts**)

COMMERCE

NOUN A **merchant account** is a type of bank account that allows a company to accept credit cards.

○ Getting a merchant account to handle credit card payments may be your best long-term solution to the problem of getting paid.

○ If you are taking credit card details over a website, you will need a merchant account with a reputable bank to process the payments.

m

mer|chant fees /mɜrtʃənt fiz/

COMMERCE

NOUN **Merchant fees** are money charged by a merchant service to a vendor for processing credit card transactions.

○ Merchant fees are calculated as a percentage of each credit card sale.

○ The Director of Sales and Marketing said that credit card merchant fees were a significant and increasing cost to the company.

mer|chant ser|vice /mɜrtʃənt sɜrvɪs/ (**merchant services**)

COMMERCE

NOUN A **merchant service** is a provider of credit card processing services.

○ In addition to banks, there are specific companies, often called merchant service companies, that offer credit card processing services.

○ The merchant service charge is a fee that retailers or merchants who accept Visa cards pay to their acquiring bank.

mod|i|fi|ca|tion /mɒdɪfɪkeɪʃᵊn/ (**modifications**)

BASIC

NOUN A **modification** is a change to the terms of a contract that have previously been agreed.

○ *The terms of loans may be regulated, with modifications from time to time so as to discourage or encourage new borrowing.*

○ *Many homeowners have reported that their lenders won't give them a mortgage modification unless they're behind on their payments.*

M

Nn

---

ne|go|tia|ble /nɪɡoʊʃiəbᵊl/

COMMERCE

ADJECTIVE A **negotiable** asset is able to be transferred legally from one owner to another.

○ Negotiable paper is a document that can be traded for value by its holder independent of the parties that created it.

○ When a negotiable paper is traded, often people will obtain it improperly and sell it to innocent buyers.

---

net¹ /nɛt/

BASIC

ADJECTIVE The **net** amount of something is the amount that remains after subtracting taxes, expenses, losses, and costs.

○ Net investment is gross investment less depreciation.

○ The net gain on the sale is the gain after subtracting the costs of sale.

▶ **COLLOCATIONS:**
net amount
net revenue
net total

---

net² /nɛt/ (nets, netted, netting)

FINANCIAL STATEMENTS

VERB If you **net** a source of income and a source of expenditure, you deduct one from the other so that you receive the difference of the two amounts.

○ *If you net debt against cash, the firm would have $200 million.*

○ *If the company settles on buying its denim in Britain because the cloth is cheapest there, the total value of the jeans that it sells in that market should be netted against its denim purchases.*

---

net as|sets /nɛt æsɛts/

FINANCIAL STATEMENTS: BALANCE SHEET

NOUN **Net assets** are the total assets of a company minus the total liabilities.

○ *These acquisitions have trebled the company's net assets over the past year.*

○ *The company said in July it would receive $25 million for the business, but the price was increased because the net assets appreciated in value.*

---

net as|set val|ue (ABBR **NAV**) /nɛt æsɛt vælyu/

FINANCIAL STATEMENTS: BALANCE SHEET

NOUN The **net asset value** is the total value of a company's assets, after subtracting any money it still owes.

○ *The sale price will range from $13 million to $15 million, depending on the net asset value of the assets being acquired on the transaction's closing date.*

○ *The net asset value of a fund is the value of its assets less its liabilities divided by the number of shares outstanding.*

---

net earn|ings /nɛt ɜrnɪŋz/

FINANCIAL STATEMENTS: INCOME STATEMENT

NOUN The **net earnings** of a person or a company is what remains of their earnings after all taxes and expenses have been subtracted.

○ *In recent years, the Fed has had net earnings after expenses of over $15 billion dollars per year.*

○ *The group has just reported a 70 percent drop in net earnings for its latest financial year.*

net in|come /nɛt ɪnkʌm/

FINANCIAL STATEMENTS: INCOME STATEMENT

NOUN **Net income** is the difference between gross profit on sales and operating expenses if gross profit is more than operating expenses.

○ Fiscal second-quarter net income tripled to $75,000 on an 11 percent sales increase.

○ Credit cards should enhance your personal financial management, and this can be done if you limit the amount outstanding to an affordable percentage of your monthly net income.

net loss /nɛt lɔs/ (**net losses**)

FINANCIAL STATEMENTS: INCOME STATEMENT

NOUN A **net loss** is the difference between gross profit on sales and operating expenses if gross profit is less than operating expenses.

○ Net loss is subtracted from the capital account, because it is treated as a deduction in the statement of owner's equity.

○ They have posted second-quarter net income of $1.7 million, or 15 cents a share, compared with a net loss of $2.3 million a year earlier.

net pre|sent val|ue (ABBR **NPV**) /nɛt prɛzᵊnt vælyu/

MANAGEMENT

NOUN The **net present value** of an investment or project is all the income that it can be expected to produce minus all the costs, taking into account the future value of this income and these costs.

○ Losses or negative returns must get subtracted from future profits or gains to calculate the net present value of the company to investors.

○ If the net present value of the project is above zero, the project is likely to be profitable.

net prof|it (INFORMAL **the net**) /nɛt prɒfɪt/

FINANCIAL STATEMENTS: INCOME STATEMENT

NOUN A company's **net profit** is its profit after subtracting all costs.

○ Net profit is what's left over after subtracting fixed expenses from gross profit.

○ As interest rates have shown signs of weakening, this will help in keeping net profit levels higher than in the preceding half-year.

net re|al|iz|a|ble val|ue (ABBR **NRV**) /nɛt riəlaɪzəbəl vælyu/

FINANCIAL STATEMENTS

NOUN The **net realizable value** of an asset is the value of the asset if it is sold, after subtracting all the costs connected with the sale.

○ Net realizable value is the current selling price less the costs of completing and selling the product.

○ The value of the buildings is the net current replacement cost, or, if there has been a recognized permanent fall in the value of the asset, the net realizable value.

net sales /nɛt seɪlz/

FINANCIAL STATEMENTS: INCOME STATEMENT

NOUN **Net sales** are total sales after subtracting discounts, returned goods, and allowances for damaged goods.

○ On the income statement of a merchandising company, cost of goods sold is deducted from net sales to arrive at gross profit.

○ The company's profits before tax constituted 31.26 percent of its net sales.

nor|mal bal|ance /nɔrməl bæləns/ (**normal balances**)

FINANCIAL STATEMENTS

NOUN The **normal balance** of an account is the side of the account that is positive or increasing.

○ The normal balance for asset and expense accounts is the debit side, while for income, equity, and liability accounts it is the credit side.

○ An account's assigned normal balance is on the side where increases go because the increases in any account are usually greater than the decreases.

note pay|a|ble /noʊt peɪəbəl/ (**notes payable**)

FINANCIAL STATEMENTS: BALANCE SHEET

NOUN A **note payable** is a written legal obligation to repay an amount of borrowed money at a particular future date.

○ As of June 30, the company had $338.8 million in short-term debt, including notes payable of $83.6 million.

○ The Company had $333,617 and $357,552 outstanding under a long-term note payable to a bank on August 31.

Oo

---

off /ɔf/

FINANCIAL STATEMENTS: BALANCE SHEET

ADJECTIVE If an amount or figure is **off**, it differs from or is inconsistent with the correct amount.

○ *The reconciliation is off by $510.37.*

○ *For a budget surplus of $234 billion in 2004, the calculation could be off by $250 billion.*

---

of|fer /ɔfər/ (offers)

COMMERCE

NOUN An **offer** is the amount of money that someone says they will pay to buy something.

○ *The company accepted a takeover offer of $29.835 a share.*

○ *They made an offer for all shares outstanding, which was approved by 80 percent of holders.*

> **TALKING ABOUT OFFERS**
>
> If you suggest an offer, you **table** it, and if you make a formal offer, you **submit** it.
>
> If you agree to an offer, you **accept** it, and if you do not agree, you **reject**, **decline**, or **refuse** it.
>
> If you change an offer you have made, you **revise** it, and if you take it away, you **withdraw** it.
>
> You can describe an offer as **conditional** if it depends on something, or you can say that an offer is **subject to** certain conditions.

on ac|count /ɒn əkount/

COMMERCE

PHRASE If you buy something **on account**, it is charged to your account, and the vendor will invoice you for it later.

○ The usual procedure for most businesses is to buy on account, rather than for cash.

○ The amount by which recorded turnover is in excess of payments on account should be classified as "amounts recoverable on contracts."

▶ **COLLOCATION:**
payment on on account

op|er|at|ing budg|et /ɒpəreɪtɪŋ bʌdʒɪt/ (**operating budgets**)

MANAGEMENT

NOUN An **operating budget** is a forecast of the costs and profits of an organization, used to monitor its trading activities, usually for one year.

○ The division's annual operating budget of about $245 million is under constant strain.

○ Six years ago, she used her savings to get the company going; this year the operating budget is $3.2m.

op|er|at|ing cost /ɒpəreɪtɪŋ kɒst/ (**operating costs**)

MANAGEMENT

NOUN The **operating cost** of a business, or a piece of equipment or machinery is the amount of money that it costs to run it.

○ The operating cost of the airplane is only between 20 and 25 percent higher than that of an equivalent turbo-prop aircraft.

○ The installation and operating cost of the system should not exceed its value to the firm.

op|er|at|ing ex|pens|es /ɒpəreɪtɪŋ ɪkspɛnsɪz/

FINANCIAL STATEMENTS: INCOME STATEMENT

NOUN **Operating expenses** are expenses related to carrying out normal business activities.

○ The restructuring plan calls for reductions in capital-spending plans and sharp cuts in operating expenses including research and development and advertising.

○ Coffee bars are very high cost models with huge rents and operating expenses.

---

op|er|at|ing in|come /ˌɒpəreɪtɪŋ ɪnkʌm/

FINANCIAL STATEMENTS: INCOME STATEMENT

NOUN **Operating income** is income earned from normal business activities.

○ The company has no leverage and all the operating income is paid as dividends to the common stockholders.

○ Half the company's operating income comes from its foreign operations, and 70 percent of that from Asia.

---

op|er|at|ing mar|gin /ˌɒpəreɪtɪŋ mɑːdʒɪn/ (**operating margins**)

MANAGEMENT

NOUN An **operating margin** is a ratio used to measure how well a company controls its costs, that is calculated by dividing operating income by net sales, and expressing it as a percentage.

○ They plan to reverse the company's decline by adding 1m in sales by October this year, achieving an operating margin of 8 percent and eliminating its debt.

○ The firm is likely to make post-tax profits of more than $1 billion this year, with a healthy operating margin of 10.7 percent.

---

op|er|at|ing prof|it /ˌɒpəreɪtɪŋ prɒfɪt/

MANAGEMENT

NOUN **Operating profit** is profit earned from normal business activities.

○ A company in control of gross margin and operating expenses will show increased operating profit.

○ The company's operating profit is only 2.1 percent of sales.

---

op|por|tu|ni|ty cost /ˌɒpətuːnɪti kɒst/ (**opportunity costs**)

MANAGEMENT

NOUN An **opportunity cost** is the cost of not being able to do other things with time and resources because of doing the chosen activity.

○ Business school applications have surged this year, though this partly reflects the economic downturn, which reduces the opportunity cost of taking time out from a career to study.

○ The opportunity cost of holding money rather than buying bonds or some other interest-bearing asset is the nominal interest that would otherwise be earned.

op|tion /ɒpʃᵊn/ (options)

INVESTING

NOUN An **option** is an agreement or contract that gives someone the right to buy or sell a property or shares at a future date.

○ Each bank has granted the other an option on 19.9 percent of its shares.

○ Under the program, he still holds options to buy 42,000 shares at the same low rate.

or|der¹ /ɔrdər/ (orders, ordered, ordering)

COMMERCE

VERB When you **order** something that you are going to pay for, you ask for it to be brought or sent to you.

○ They are depleting their stock on hand before ordering new inventory.

○ Stores order their merchandise for the critical Christmas season in the summer.

or|der² /ɔrdər/ (orders)

COMMERCE

NOUN Someone's **order** is a usually written request to purchase the goods or services listed.

○ There has been a rise in orders for business plant and equipment.

○ Sagging demand for cars held down orders for transportation equipment.

or|di|nar|y gain /ɔrdᵊnɛri geɪn/ (ordinary gains)

TAX

NOUN An **ordinary gain** is a gain in the course of normal business.

○ Foreign currency gain or loss is calculated separately from any gain or loss on the underlying transaction, and is normally taxable as ordinary gain or loss.

○ Taxpayers are required to treat all gain as ordinary gain unless the property is sold for more than its original cost.

or|di|nar|y loss /ˈɔrdᵊnɛri lɔs/ (ordinary losses)

TAX

NOUN An **ordinary loss** is a loss in the course of normal business.

○ When the company became insolvent, his loss on the stock was not a capital loss but a fully deductible ordinary loss.

○ In general, any net gain from the sale or conversion of such assets is regarded as long-term capital gain; any net loss, as an ordinary loss, deductible in full.

oth|er ex|pens|es /ˈʌðər ɪksˈpɛnsɪz/

FINANCIAL STATEMENTS: INCOME STATEMENT

NOUN **Other expenses** are expenses that do not relate to a company's main business.

○ As well as operating costs, the company needs to consider other expenses including interest expense and losses from disposing of fixed assets.

○ Examples of other expenses include interest expense and losses from disposing of fixed assets.

oth|er in|come /ˈʌðər ɪnkʌm/

FINANCIAL STATEMENTS: INCOME STATEMENT

NOUN **Other income** is income that does not come from a company's main business, such as interest.

○ Examples of other income include income from interest, rent, and gains resulting from the sale of fixed assets.

○ Companies present other income in a separate section, before income from operations.

out|stand|ing /aʊtstændɪŋ/
BASIC

ADJECTIVE Money that is **outstanding** has not yet been paid and is still owed to someone.

○ The total debt outstanding is $70 billion.

○ The company had 140.9 million shares outstanding in the latest quarter.

o|ver|head /oʊvərhɛd/ (overheads)
MANAGEMENT

COUNT/NONCOUNT NOUN **Overheads** are the regular and essential expenses of running a business, such as salaries, rent, and bills.

○ We are having to reduce overheads to remain competitive.

○ The anticipated growth in earnings will come partly from significantly higher orders, as well as from major reductions in overhead and expenses.

o|ver|stat|ed /oʊvərsteɪtɪd/
FINANCIAL STATEMENTS

ADJECTIVE If an account or a figure on an account is **overstated**, the amount that is reported on the financial statement is more than it should be.

○ Auditors will be asking the company's directors to explain why non-current assets in the accounts were overstated and not reported at their recoverable amount.

○ For fiscal 2010, they reported preproduction costs of $55.4 million, which was overstated by approximately $4 million.

o

Pp

---

pack|ing slip /pǽkɪŋ slɪp/ (packing slips)

COMMERCE

NOUN A **packing slip** is a list of what is included in a shipment.

○ When we write up the order, we write up the invoice for pricing, the packing slip for shipping the finished product, and the work order showing what needs to be done.

○ The document that tells the shipping department to release inventory for delivery is usually the packing slip.

---

paid-in cap|i|tal /peɪd ɪn kǽpɪtᵊl/

FINANCIAL STATEMENTS: BALANCE SHEET

NOUN **Paid-in capital** is the money a company has received from investors in return for issuing stock.

○ Paid-in capital arising from the sale of treasury stock should not be included in the measurement of net income.

○ The price of new shares sold to the public almost always exceeds the par value, and the difference is entered in the company's accounts as additional paid-in capital or capital surplus.

---

part|ner|ship /pɑ́rtnərʃɪp/ (partnerships)

BASIC

NOUN A **partnership** is a company that is owned by two or more people, who share in the risks and rewards of the business.

○ The department store operator said that buying the stake in the subsidiary is part of a broad agreement to form a partnership.

○ When the two companies merged, the bigger company became the dominant player in the partnership.

p

past due /pæst du/

COMMERCE

ADJECTIVE If an amount of money owed is **past due**, it is still owing beyond the payment date.

○ Several contractors terminated construction, because progress payments were past due.

○ Under terms of the debentures, the company can't redeem the bonds if certain of its debt is past due.

pay|ee /peɪi/ (payees)

COMMERCE

NOUN A **payee** is a person who is to receive money.

○ On the check, write the name of the payee and then sign your name.

○ Where a check is cleared through a bank, the drawer's account is debited with the amount involved and the payee's account is credited with it.

pay|ment in ad|vance /peɪmənt ɪn ædvæns/ (payments in advance)

COMMERCE

NOUN If a business asks for **payment in advance**, the payment must be received in full before the goods or services are delivered.

○ Manufacturers typically require either payment in advance or a letter of credit from a bank.

○ The company has the right to require payment in advance or an acceptable guarantee of payment from those who seem unlikely to be able to pay.

pay|or /peɪɔr/ (payors)

COMMERCE

NOUN A **payor** is a person who makes a payment.

○ Where tax advice is given in a divorce settlement and one spouse pays the fees for the attorneys of both spouses, the payor cannot deduct both fees as legal fees.

○ The float period is the time between when a check is written and when it clears the payor's checking account.

> **WORD BUILDER**
>
> **-or** = person that does something
>
> The suffix **-or** often appears in words for people who do a particular thing: **auditor**, **creditor**, **debtor**, **lessor**, **payor**, **vendor**.

---

pe|ri|od costs /pɪəriəd kɔsts/

MANAGEMENT

NOUN **Period costs** are general costs that cannot be associated with a particular product, such as utilities or insurance.

○ Our gross margins at any point in time include both the direct product costs and also some period costs.

○ Period costs are all nonproduct expenditures for managing the firm and selling the product.

---

per|ma|nent ac|count /pɜrmənənt əkaʊnt/ (**permanent accounts**)

FINANCIAL STATEMENTS: BALANCE SHEET

NOUN A **permanent account** is an account which carries its balance and is kept open from year to year.

○ The period-ending balance in a permanent account is carried forward into the next accounting period as that period's beginning balance.

○ The retained earnings account, like all other balance sheet accounts, is a permanent account because its ending balance from one year becomes its beginning balance for the following year.

---

per|son|al prop|er|ty /pɜrsənᵊl prɒpərti/

BASIC

NOUN A person's or a company's **personal property** is their assets other than land and buildings.

○ The property tax is levied on personal property, such as cars and boats, as well as on residential and commercial real estate.

○ Personal property refers to tangible items that are not permanently attached to or part of the real estate.

pet|ty cash /pɛti kæʃ/

BASIC

NOUN **Petty cash** is money that is kept in the office of a company, for making small payments in cash when necessary.

○ *After having her expense claims overruled, she took the money from petty cash.*

○ *Companies normally use checks to pay their obligations because checks provide a record of each payment, but they also maintain a petty cash fund to pay for small, miscellaneous expenditures.*

plant /plænt/

MANAGEMENT

NOUN A **plant** is a factory, or a place where power is produced.

○ *About 90 percent of the company's hair-care products come from plants in China.*

○ *The manufacturing plant was struggling to break even due to high inventories.*

post /poʊst/ (posts, posted, posting)

FINANCIAL STATEMENTS

VERB If you **post** a transaction or result, you report it, or enter it in an account.

○ *Both banks are expected to announce huge further write-downs when they post fourth-quarter results next week.*

○ *The stocks of large U.S. companies continued to post tremendous returns as investors poured money into U.S. equities.*

post|date /poʊstdeɪt/ (postdates, postdated, postdating)

COMMERCE

VERB If you **postdate** a check or other document, you put a future date on it so that it is not valid until then.

○ *It is inadvisable for a payee to take a postdated check in satisfaction of an outstanding debt.*

○ *Postdated checks were used instead of bills of exchange payable at fixed future dates during periods in which the stamp duty on checks was lower than on bills.*

P|P|E /piː piː iː/ (short for **property, plant and equipment**)

FINANCIAL STATEMENTS

ABBREVIATION **PPE** is a classification on a balance sheet of a company's fixed assets, such as buildings, computers, furniture, land, and machinery, that are expected to be used for more than a year.

○ PPE is shown on the balance sheet grouped together at original cost, minus net accumulated depreciation.

○ PPE are tangible items that are expected to be used during more than one period and are used in the production or supply of goods or services, for rental to others, or for administrative purposes.

pref|erred stock /prɪfɜːd stɒk/

INVESTING

NOUN **Preferred stock** is the shares in a company that are owned by people who have the right to receive part of the company's profits before the holders of common stock.

○ They approved the proposal to swap one share of preferred stock for 1.2 shares of common stock and one warrant to purchase another common share for $3.50 until June 30.

○ The options entitle the employees to purchase preferred stock at $50 per share.

pre|paid ex|pense /priːpeɪd ɪkspɛns/ (**prepaid expenses**)

FINANCIAL STATEMENTS: BALANCE SHEET

NOUN A **prepaid expense** is an expense that has been paid for before it is incurred, and that is treated as an asset.

○ A prepaid expense is paid first and expensed later.

○ Prepaid expenses are assets because they relate to expenditures made which have future economic benefit.

pre|pay|ment /priːpeɪmənt/ (**prepayments**)

COMMERCE

COUNT/NONCOUNT NOUN A **prepayment** is a payment that you make before you receive goods or services, or before a debt is due.

○ *If a borrower makes prepayments, the loan balance declines more rapidly than would otherwise be possible.*

○ *During periods of rising interest rates, the rate of prepayments generally declines.*

---

pre|sent val|ue of fu|ture cash flows /prɛzənt vælyu əv fyu̠tʃər kæʃ flouz/

BASIC

NOUN The **present value of future cash flows** is a method of discounting cash that you expect to receive in the future to the value at the current time.

○ *They use information about the degree of risk associated with any investment to derive a discount rate appropriate for estimating the present value of future cash flows, which is the basis of most asset pricing models.*

○ *If no comparable market prices exist, the present value of future cash flows should be used as a measure of fair value.*

▶ SYNONYM:
discounted value of future cash flows

---

price /praɪs/ (prices)

BASIC

NOUN The **price** of something is the amount of money that you have to pay in order to buy it.

○ *It was alleged that they sold securities at a loss and then repurchased them by prior agreement at the same or slightly higher prices.*

○ *There are still big variations in the prices charged for the same car model in different European countries.*

> **TALKING ABOUT PRICES**
>
> If you make prices higher, you **increase** or **raise** them, and if you make them lower, you **cut**, **lower**, or **reduce** them. If you say that prices are **slashed**, you mean they have been cut a lot.
>
> If prices are getting higher, you can say they are **rising** or **soaring**, and if they are getting lower, you can say they are **falling**.
>
> If you **quote** a price, you say you will do something or sell something for that price, and if you **charge** a price, that is how much someone must pay you.

If you decide how much things should cost, you **set** prices. If something is sold for a particular amount, it **fetches** that price.

To talk about how much things cost, you can say that prices **start at** a particular amount, or that prices **range from** one amount **to** another.

The **retail** price for something is the amount it costs in a store, and the **wholesale** price is the amount it costs to buy a large quantity of it.

price earn|ings ra|ti|o (ABBR **PE ratio**) /praɪs ɜrnɪŋz reɪʃoʊ/
INVESTING

NOUN The **price earnings ratio** is the market price of common stock per share divided by earnings per share.

○ The price earnings ratio is the most widely used valuation method, comparing the ratio of the current stock price to the current or projected earnings per share.

○ The price earnings ratio relates market values to company profits.

prime cost /praɪm kɔst/ (**prime costs**)
MANAGEMENT

NOUN A **prime cost** is the part of the cost of a commodity that changes according to the amount of it that is produced, such as materials and labor.

○ The total cost of production is divided into prime cost, works cost, and cost of production.

○ Prime costs are the primary costs of production; the sum of the direct materials costs and direct labor costs.

prin|ci|pal /prɪnsɪpᵊl/ (**principals**)
INVESTING

NOUN A **principal** is the amount of money originally borrowed on a loan.

○ The agreement gives bank creditors three basic options: cutting back interest payments, reducing debt principal, or lending further funds.

○ Investors have the choice of having not just the principal, but also the dividends cumulatively being converted into shares.

pro|ceeds /proʊsidz/
BASIC

NOUN The **proceeds** of an activity or the sale of something is the money and other assets received from it.

○ *The company planned to use the proceeds from the sale to help pay the debt it would have incurred in its proposed $12 billion acquisition.*

○ *They reached an agreement that they won't pursue a claim to the proceeds of the planned sale.*

prod|uct /prɒdʌkt/ (**products**)
BASIC

NOUN A **product** is something that you manufacture or grow in order to sell it.

○ *This cellphone is one of the company's most successful products.*

○ *The steelmaker was hurt by holding higher-cost inventory when raw material costs of such key products as nickel dropped.*

prod|uct costs /prɒdʌkt kɔsts/
MANAGEMENT

NOUN **Product costs** are costs that can be directly associated with a particular product, such as manufacturing and sales costs.

○ *Cost of sales consists of direct product costs such as materials, labor, cost of warranty, and depreciation.*

○ *We are continuously challenged to find new ways of lowering product costs in order to maximize returns.*

pro|duc|tion /prədʌkʃən/
MANAGEMENT

NOUN **Production** is the process of making or growing something in large amounts, or the amount of goods that you make or grow.

○ *This car went into production last year.*

○ *The factory has shown itself able to increase production as demand rises.*

> **TALKING ABOUT PRODUCTION**
>
> We say that production **increases** or **rises** or that it **declines** or **falls**.
>
> If people try to increase production, they **stimulate**, **boost**, or **expand** it.
>
> If they **halt** or **cease** production, they stop it, and if they **resume** production, they start it again.
>
> If a company **shifts** production to a different place, they move their factories there.
>
> **Domestic** production is products that are made within a country.

---

prof|it /prɒfɪt/ (profits)

BASIC

NOUN **Profit** is the amount by which revenues are more than expenses in a business enterprise over a given period of time.

○ *Exports produce the bulk of corporate profits, even though domestic consumption accounts for about 60 percent of GDP.*

○ *The bank made pre-tax profits of $6.5 million.*

> **PROFITS**
>
> The following are words connected with receiving profit and income:
>
> capital gain, earnings, gain on sale, margin, receipts, surplus, yield

---

prof|it|a|bil|i|ty /prɒfɪtəbɪlɪti/

BASIC

NOUN A company's **profitability** is its ability to make a profit.

○ *Changes were made in operating methods in an effort to increase profitability.*

○ *Management needs to introduce efficient processes to increase productivity and to drive profitability upwards.*

prof|it and loss state|ment (ABBR **P&L**) /prɒfɪt ənd lɔs steɪtmənt/ (**profit and loss statements**)

FINANCIAL STATEMENTS: INCOME STATEMENT

NOUN A **profit and loss statement** is a statement that is compiled at the end of a financial year showing that year's revenue and expense items and indicating gross and net profit or loss.

○ The profit and loss statement is a summary of the business income after expenses are paid.

○ A cash budget is solely concerned with the timing of cash receipts and payments during a period, whereas a profit and loss statement is concerned with the revenue and expenses which accrue during a period.

prof|it cen|ter /prɒfɪt sɛntər/ (**profit centers**)

MANAGEMENT

NOUN A **profit center** is a part of a company that is responsible for its own costs and profits.

○ Now that each profit center has to pay salaries, managers aren't so happy to take more workers than they need.

○ A profit center is an organizational subunit of a firm which is given responsibility for minimizing operating costs and maximizing revenue within its limited sphere of operations.

prof|it mar|gin /prɒfɪt mɑrdʒɪn/ (**profit margins**)

MANAGEMENT

NOUN A **profit margin** is the difference between the selling price of a product and the cost of producing and marketing it.

○ Profit margins measure how much a company earns in relation to its overall sales and, generally, the higher they are, the more efficient the company is.

○ Firms have tended to increase their profit margins on existing volumes, rather than cut prices to increase their market share.

pro for|ma /proʊ fɔrmə/

FINANCIAL STATEMENTS

ADJECTIVE A company's **pro forma** balance or earnings are their expected balance or earnings.

○ Companies seeking debt financing usually draw up a set of pro forma income statements and balance sheets.

○ The company presented its pro forma earnings as if it had not paid $4 million in payroll taxes and, had not lost $7 million investing in poor stocks.

---

prom|is|so|ry note /prɒmɪsɔri noʊt/ (**promissory notes**)
INVESTING

NOUN A **promissory note** is a written promise to pay a particular sum of money to someone by a particular date.

○ If an order is very large, the customer may be asked to sign a promissory note.

○ The borrower must signal their good faith by making a deposit or signing a promissory note or letter of credit guaranteed by the central bank.

---

pro ra|ta /proʊ reɪtə/
BASIC

ADJECTIVE Something that is **pro rata** is allocated in proportion to its share of the whole.

○ Each company in the group pays its pro rata share of losses and expenses.

○ They are paid their salaries and are entitled to fringe benefits on a pro rata basis.

---

pro|vi|sion /prəvɪʒᵊn/ (**provisions**)
BASIC

COUNT/NONCOUNT NOUN A **provision** is an estimated amount set aside for a liability such as bad debt or income tax where the exact amount of a particular liability is uncertain.

○ Pretax profits before debt provisions rose 13 percent to a record $937 million.

○ The provision would reduce the amount of losses that can be carried back for tax purposes by corporations that replace equity with debt.

---

pub|lic com|pa|ny /pʌblɪk kʌmpəni/ (**public companies**)
INVESTING

NOUN A **public company** is a company whose shares can be bought by the general public.

○ *Shares in a public company can be bought and sold on the stock exchange and so can be bought by the general public.*

○ *A public company is usually defined as one whose shares are sold or issued to the public and which must have at least two directors.*

▶ **SYNONYM:**
publicly traded company

---

pur|chase ledg|er /pɜrtʃɪs lɛdʒər/ (**purchase ledgers**)

FINANCIAL STATEMENTS

NOUN A **purchase ledger** is a record of a company's purchases of goods and services showing the amounts that have been paid and remain to be paid.

○ *The purchase ledger exceeds the value of the sales ledger as at September 30 by nearly $300 thousand.*

○ *This system will ensure that correct spend is entered in the purchase ledger after goods receipt and the supplier gets paid without further manual intervention.*

---

pur|chase or|der /pɜrtʃɪs ɔrdər/ (**purchase orders**)

COMMERCE

NOUN A **purchase order** is a written list of the goods or services that a person or company wants to purchase.

○ *Each fund reserves the right to reject any purchase order, and if a purchase is canceled because your check is returned unpaid, you are responsible for any loss incurred.*

○ *A purchase order is a written request to a supplier for specified goods at an agreed-upon price.*

P

Qq

quick ra|ti|o /kwɪk reɪʃoʊ/

NOUN A **quick ratio** is a measure of liquidity that is calculated by dividing current assets minus inventories by current liabilities.

○ *The current ratio and the quick ratio help investors determine whether companies have enough coverage to meet near-term cash requirements.*

○ *The quick ratio is calculated as total receivables plus cash and all securities readily transferable into cash, divided by total current liabilities.*

▶ **SYNONYM:**
acid test

RATIOS

The following are all types of ratio that are used in accounting:

asset turnover ratio, current ratio, debt-to-equity ratio, price earnings ratio, quick ratio

---

q

quote /kwoʊt/ (quotes)

NOUN A **quote for** a piece of work is the price that someone says they will charge you to do the work.

○ *Always get a written quote for any repairs needed.*

○ *Negotiate the cost of a trade-in after you have the lowest quote for the car in writing.*

Rr

---

rate of re|turn /reɪt əv rɪtɜrn/

NOUN The **rate of return** on an investment is the amount of profit that the investment makes.

○ High rates of return can be earned on these investments.

○ While there are no fixed rates of return, the yields on these units broadly reflect the interest rates prevailing in the market.

---

raw ma|te|ri|als /rɔ mətɪəriəlz/

NOUN **Raw materials** are materials that are in their natural state, before they are processed or used in manufacturing.

○ These ships bring the raw materials for the ever-expanding textile industry.

○ It is important to integrate and synchronize all the functions that must be performed in order to convert raw materials into finished products.

▶ **SYNONYM:**
direct materials

---

real es|tate /ril ɪsteɪt/

NOUN **Real estate** is property in the form of land and buildings.

○ Purchases of foreign real estate, such as rental houses, for non-business purposes will remain prohibited.

○ The law is supposed to bring more real estate into productive usage for housing.

re|al|ized gains /ríəlaɪzd geɪz/

FINANCIAL STATEMENTS: INCOME STATEMENT

NOUN **Realized gains** are gains which have been made from the sale of an asset.

○ Payments will be made to mutual fund shareholders of realized gains from the sale of a fund's portfolio securities.

○ Realized gains arise from the sale of assets during the accounting period.

re|al|ized loss|es /ríəlaɪzd lɔsɪz/

FINANCIAL STATEMENTS: INCOME STATEMENT

NOUN **Realized losses** are losses which have occurred upon the sale of an asset.

○ When funds have net realized losses, investors can carry those forward for up to eight years and use them to offset realized gains later in that period.

○ The discontinued operation reported operating losses of $60000 and realized losses on the disposal of assets of $35000.

real prop|er|ty /ríl prɒpərti/

BASIC

NOUN **Real property** is land, buildings, and anything attached to the land.

○ Not only is your house real property, but so is the light fitting that hangs from the ceiling.

○ Real property is land and objects attached to land in a relatively permanent manner; personal property is property not classified as real.

r

re|ceipt /rɪsíːt/ (**receipts**)

COMMERCE

NOUN A **receipt** is a written statement that shows that you have received goods or money.

○ I wrote her a receipt for the money.

○ In order to collect, the company must prove through accounting records or receipts that fraud occurred.

re|ceipts /rɪsi̱ts/

COMMERCE

NOUN **Receipts** are the amount of money that is received by a business during a particular period of time.

○ The company will continue to donate a portion of its receipts to charity under its Good Neighbor program.

○ Squeezed by falling revenue receipts and ballooning expenditure, borrowings skyrocketed in 2009–2010.

re|ceiv|a|bles /rɪsi̱vəbᵊlz/

COMMERCE

NOUN **Receivables** are amounts of money owing to you that can be collected on.

○ The group might have to write off as much as $200 million in bad inventory and uncollectable receivables.

○ In an effort to manage working capital better, the company is looking strictly at inventories, payables, and receivables.

re|ceiv|a|bles col|lec|tion pe|ri|od /rɪsi̱vəbᵊlz kəlɛ̱kʃᵊn pɪə̱riəd/ (**receivables collection periods**)

MANAGEMENT

NOUN A **receivables collection period** is a measure of cash flow that is calculated by dividing average receivables by credit sales per day.

○ Their lean manufacturing and relatively short receivables collection period has resulted in a significant level of liquidity.

○ The receivables collection period measures the number of days it takes, on average, to collect accounts receivable based on the average balance in accounts receivable.

▶ SYNONYMS:
average collection period
days sales outstanding

re|ceiv|a|bles turn|o|ver /rɪsivəbᵊlz tɜrnoʊvər/

MANAGEMENT

NOUN A **receivables turnover** is a measure of cash flow that is calculated by dividing net credit sales by average accounts receivable.

○ The receivables turnover figures show the ratio of sales to the accounts receivable balance.

○ Managers, directors, investors, and creditors evaluate the effectiveness of a company's credit-granting and collection activities by conducting a receivables turnover analysis.

re|ceiv|er /rɪsivər/ (receivers)

COMMERCE

NOUN A **receiver** is a document recording the quantity and condition of goods when they are received by the buyer.

○ Invoices will not be approved for payment without a signed purchase order, packing slip, and signed receiver attached.

○ Before the receiver is signed, all merchandise must be inspected to verify that items being delivered are in good condition and are the same item numbers and quantities as listed on the purchase order.

▶ SYNONYM:
receiving report

re|clas|si|fy /riklæsɪfaɪ/ (reclassifies, reclassified, reclassifying)

FINANCIAL STATEMENTS

VERB If you **reclassify** a transaction, you change the way in which it is classified.

○ Costs were simply reclassified as capital expenses to boost cash flow and profits.

○ Capital gains tax deters people from trying to avoid income tax by reclassifying income as capital gains.

> **WORD BUILDER**
> **re-** = again
>
> The prefix **re-** often appears in words that relate to doing something again: **reclassify**, **refund**, **reimburse**.

rec|og|nize /ˈrɛkəgnaɪz/ (recognizes, recognized, recognizing)

BASIC

VERB If you **recognize** a transaction, you record it as occurring in a particular period.

○ We recognized the income from the sale in the prior quarter.

○ Changes in market value of foreign exchange contracts are recognized as gains or losses.

rec|on|cile an ac|count /ˈrɛkənsaɪl ən əˈkaʊnt/

COMMERCE

PHRASE If you **reconcile an account**, you compare the items in a bank statement, credit card statement, or vendor statement with the entries on your books and make sure that the statement and books match.

○ The government is trying to reconcile the accounts of the state-owned oil company with those of the central bank and the treasury.

○ The directors have to compare the annual and interim accounts carefully, as they could face legal action if they cannot reconcile these accounts.

re|cur|ring /rɪˈkɜrɪŋ/

BASIC

ADJECTIVE If something is **recurring**, it happens at regularly occurring intervals.

○ More than 60 percent of recurring costs were attributable directly to materials, products, and services purchased from external suppliers.

○ Include in the expenses accrued for the period all recurring fees that are charged to all shareholder accounts in proportion to the length of the base period.

re|fund /ˈrifʌnd/ (refunds, refunded, refunding)

COMMERCE

VERB If someone **refunds** your money, they return what you have paid them.

○ We will refund your delivery costs if the items arrive later than 12 noon.

○ We guarantee to refund your money if you're not delighted with your purchase.

reg|is|ter /rɛdʒɪstər/ (registers)

FINANCIAL STATEMENTS

NOUN A **register** is an official list of people or things.

○ He transferred information from the payroll register to the employees' earnings records.

○ You can enter a transaction directly into the register.

re|im|burse /riːmbɜrs/ (reimburses, reimbursed, reimbursing)

COMMERCE

VERB If you **reimburse** someone **for** something, you pay them back the money that they have spent or lost because of it.

○ I will be happy to reimburse you for any expenses you have had.

○ Employees will be reimbursed for paying travel expenses from their own funds.

re|mit /rɪmɪt/ (remits, remitted, remitting)

COMMERCE

VERB If you **remit** money, you send it as payment.

○ The bank must wait 21 days before remitting the money to the IRS.

○ He will be taxed in Britain on all his income, not just that which is generated domestically or remitted from abroad.

re|mit|tance ad|vice /rɪmɪtᵊns ædvaɪs/ (remittance advices)

COMMERCE

NOUN A **remittance advice** is a document that describes payments that are being made, especially the part of the invoice that the customer sends back with payment.

○ Payment is by bank credit, but staff still receive a remittance advice which confirms payment has been made.

○ The portion above the perforated line is the remittance advice, which the customer removes and returns with the payment.

r

re|port /rɪpɔ̱rt/ (reports, reported, reporting)

BASIC

VERB If a company **reports** losses or earnings, it makes a public statement detailing how much money the company has lost or earned.

○ The board of directors expect to report a substantial loss for the company's fourth quarter ended June 30.

○ The group expects to report second-quarter earnings of $1.7 million.

▶ COLLOCATIONS:
report a loss
report a profit

---

re|port|ing /rɪpɔ̱rtɪŋ/

BASIC

NOUN **Reporting** means relating to the issuing of reports.

○ A reporting entity is an organization or company, or group of companies that prepares financial reports.

○ A broker-dealer must be in compliance with the requirement to obtain current reports filed by a reporting issuer.

---

re|serve /rɪzɜ̱rv/ (reserves)

BASIC

NOUN A **reserve** is money that has been set aside for future expected expenses.

○ Legal reserve is the amount of money a bank or insurance company must keep to cover future claims and losses.

○ Banks borrow from each other, if necessary, to keep average daily reserves over a two-week period at certain minimum levels.

---

re|sid|u|al /rɪzɪ̱dʒuəl/

BASIC

ADJECTIVE A **residual** amount is an amount that is left over or remains.

○ The total depreciation to be charged over the useful life will be the difference between acquisition cost and residual value at the end of the asset's useful life.

○ *Residual income is the operating income that an investment center earns above a minimum desired return on invested assets.*

---

re|strict|ed /rɪstrɪktɪd/

BASIC

ADJECTIVE **Restricted** assets or funds are assets or funds that can only be used for a particular purpose.

○ *A scholarship fund would clearly be included among temporarily restricted net assets.*

○ *Current restricted funds are resources given to an organization to be expended for specific operating purposes.*

---

re|tail /rɪteɪl/

COMMERCE

ADJECTIVE If you talk about a **retail** business, price, or sale, you mean a business that sells goods directly to the public or a price or sale when you are selling goods directly to the public.

○ *Reimbursement will be the lower of either the retail price or the wholesale price plus $4.50.*

○ *Retail stores usually count on the Christmas season to make up to half of their annual profits.*

▶ **COLLOCATIONS:**
retail business
retail outlet
retail price
retail store

---

re|tained earn|ings /rɪteɪnd ɜrnɪŋz/

FINANCIAL STATEMENTS: BALANCE SHEET

NOUN **Retained earnings** are the profit that a company does not pay out in dividends, but keeps in order to reinvest in itself.

○ *Dividends and retained earnings come from after-tax income.*

○ *Most investment is financed within individual economic units – as when a company pays for new plant from retained earnings.*

ret|ro|ac|tive /rɛtrouˈæktɪv/

BASIC

ADJECTIVE A **retroactive** transaction applies a change to previous accounting periods.

○ There will be no retroactive adjustments in sales charges on investments previously made during the 13-month period.

○ Disclosure must be provided of any retroactive change to prior period financial statements, including the effect of any such change on income and income per share.

re|turn /rɪˈtɜrn/ (**returns**)

INVESTING

NOUN A **return** on an investment is the profit that you get from it.

○ Profits have picked up but the return on capital remains tiny.

○ Higher returns and higher risk usually go hand in hand.

re|turn of cap|i|tal /rɪˈtɜrn əv ˈkæpɪtᵊl/

INVESTING

NOUN A **return of capital** is a situation in which you receive back money that was previously invested.

○ The company may be permitted to pay a liquidating dividend, and, because such payments are regarded as a return of capital, they are not taxed as income.

○ Dividends paid shortly after the purchase of shares by an investor, although in effect a return of capital, are taxable to shareholders who are subject to tax.

re|turn on as|sets (ABBR **ROA**) /rɪˈtɜrn ɒn ˈæsɛts/

INVESTING

NOUN A **return on assets** is a measure of profitability that is calculated by dividing net income after interest and taxes by average total assets.

○ All firms would like to earn a higher return on assets, but their ability to do so is limited by competition.

○ In the U.S., the pharmaceutical sector has consistently generated the highest return on assets for the past two decades.

re|turn on cap|i|tal (ABBR **ROC**) /rɪtɜrn ɒn kæpɪtᵊl/

INVESTING

NOUN A **return on capital** is any earnings that you receive from the capital that you have invested.

○ As the total sales value is only 1.5 times the capital invested, the return on capital only works out at 15 percent.

○ The companies have greatly increased their return on capital as they have shed unproductive workers and subsidiaries or moved to low-cost locations.

re|turn on eq|ui|ty (ABBR **ROE**) /rɪtɜrn ɒn ɛkwɪti/

INVESTING

NOUN A **return on equity** is a measure of profitability that is calculated by dividing net income after interest and taxes by average common stockholders' equity.

○ The return on equity measures how well the owners are doing on their investment.

○ The company's treasury department actively takes risks in order to generate the return on equity demanded by investors.

re|turn on in|vest|ment (ABBR **ROI**) /rɪtɜrn ɒn ɪnvɛstmənt/

INVESTING

NOUN A **return on investment** is a measure of profitability that is calculated by dividing net profit by total assets.

○ Incentive plans are usually based on indicators of corporate performance, such as net income, total dividends paid, or some specific return on investment.

○ However large the potential return on investment, companies will find it hard to raise money for new plants.

rev|e|nue /rɛvənyu/

BASIC

NOUN **Revenue** is money that a company, an organization, or a government receives.

○ The company gets 98 percent of its revenue from Internet advertising.

○ They learnt how to project future revenue and profit estimates for the purpose of achieving steady growth.

rev|e|nue stream /rɛvənyu strim/ (revenue streams)

MANAGEMENT

NOUN A **revenue stream** is the money that a company receives from selling a particular product or service.

○ The events business is crucial to the group in that it provides a constant revenue stream.

○ A majority of the fund's assets are in revenue bonds, which are backed by the revenue stream of a particular project.

R

Ss

sal|a|ry /ˈsæləri/ (salaries)

BASIC

NOUN Your **salary** is the money that you earn each month from your employer.

- The retirement plan guarantees a pension based on final salary and years of service.
- Each team member receives a base salary, and shares commissions based on reaching a monthly team goal.

sales /seɪlz/

BASIC

NOUN The **sales** of a product are the quantity of it that is sold.

- The newspaper has sales of 1.72 million.
- The company expects huge Christmas sales of computer games.

sales ledg|er /seɪlz lɛdʒər/ (sales ledgers)

FINANCIAL STATEMENTS

NOUN A **sales ledger** is a record of a company's sales, showing the amounts paid and owed by customers.

- He entered the week's orders into the sales ledger.
- The sales ledger contains the individual accounts of each customer who has bought goods on credit.

S

sales slip /seɪlz slɪp/ (**sales slips**)

COMMERCE

NOUN A **sales slip** is a piece of paper that you are given when you buy something in a store, which shows when you bought it and how much you paid.

○ The sales clerk in the retail store was happy to exchange an item for a customer – with or without the sales slip.

○ If you want to return merchandise to the store, staff will insist on seeing the original sales slip.

sav|ings ac|count /seɪvɪŋz əkaʊnt/ (**savings accounts**)

INVESTING

NOUN A **savings account** is a bank account with a limited number of transactions per month and which pays a higher interest rate than a checking account.

○ Balances above a certain amount in a checking account are automatically transferred into a savings account that pays interest.

○ An emergency fund is a sum equal to six months of your present income set aside in a savings account.

S cor|po|ra|tion /ɛs kɔrpəreɪʃᵊn/ (**S corporations**)

BASIC

NOUN An **S corporation** is a type of corporation in which the owners are taxed for any taxable income on their individual returns.

○ Dealings in its own stock are not taxable to the S corporation.

○ If a corporation qualifies and chooses to become an S corporation, its income usually will be taxed to the shareholders.

se|cured /sɪkyʊərd/

BASIC

ADJECTIVE A **secured** loan or creditor has an asset such as a car or house pledged as collateral, which may be taken to satisfy the debt if the loan is not repaid.

○ Loans with collateral requirements are often referred to as secured loans.

○ Secured creditors take less risk because the credit that they extend is usually backed by collateral, such as a mortgage or other assets of the company.

---

se|cu|ri|ties /sɪkyʊərɪtiz/

INVESTING

NOUN **Securities** are financial or investment instruments that are bought and sold.

○ In a short sale, an investor sells borrowed securities, hoping to profit by buying them back later at a cheaper price.

○ Under current accounting rules, thrifts that own bonds aren't required to mark them to market value as long as they have the ability and intention to hold those securities to maturity.

---

sell|ing ex|pens|es /sɛlɪŋ ɪkspɛnsɪz/

FINANCIAL STATEMENTS: INCOME STATEMENT

NOUN **Selling expenses** are expenses that are related to sales activities, such as delivery costs and salespeople's wages.

○ Distribution expenses are largely selling expenses, such as the first-year commission, advertising, and agency allowances.

○ Although automobile sales increased in the U.S., fiercely competitive U.S. market conditions increased selling expenses, which adversely affected earnings.

▶ SYNONYM:
   expense of sales

---

ser|vic|es /sɜrvɪsɪz/

BASIC

NOUN **Services** are activities such as tourism, banking, and accountancy that are part of a country's economy, but are not concerned with producing or manufacturing goods.

○ The company uses the accrual basis of accounting and recognizes revenue at the time it sells products or renders services.

○ The current account, or balance of payments, is a measure of trade in goods and services and certain other transactions.

S

set off /sɛt ɔf/ (sets off, set off, setting off)

VERB If you **set off** a debit on one account against a credit on another, you deduct the debit from the credit so that the figure you receive is the difference of the two amounts.

○ The reporting party has the right to set off the amount payable, by contract or other agreement, with the amount receivable.

○ Amounts representing assets should not be set off against amounts representing liabilities.

share /ʃɛər/ (shares)

NOUN A **share** is one of the equal parts that the value of a company is divided into and that you can buy as an investment.

○ I've bought shares in my brother's new company.

○ People in China are eager to buy shares in new businesses.

share|hold|er /ʃɛərhoʊldər/ (shareholders)

NOUN A **shareholder** is an investor who owns one or more shares of stock in a company.

○ Under the plan, shareholders will exchange their common stock for an equal number of shares in the new holding company.

○ From the proceeds, the company said it will declare a distribution of $7.50 a share to its shareholders.

▶ **SYNONYM:**
stockholder

share|holders' eq|ui|ty /ʃɛərhoʊldərz ɛkwɪti/

NOUN **Shareholders' equity** is the total amount of ownership investment in a company.

○ Shareholders' equity is comprised of all capital contributed to the entity including paid-in capital and retained earnings.

○ In its most common form, shareholders' equity includes the shareholders' original investment plus those earnings of the corporation that have been retained for internal expansion rather than paid out to shareholders as dividends.

ship|ment /ʃɪpmənt/ (shipments)

COMMERCE

COUNT/NONCOUNT NOUN A **shipment** is all of the goods being shipped together at the same time.

○ If regular shipments are made, an open-cargo policy can be used that insures the goods automatically when they are shipped.

○ After that, food shipments to the port could begin in a matter of weeks.

ship|ping doc|u|ments /ʃɪpɪŋ dɒkyəmənts/

COMMERCE

NOUN **Shipping documents** are forms that accompany a shipment listing the date shipped, the customer, the method of shipment, and the quantities and specifications of goods shipped.

○ For bulk shipments of products, the lot number should appear on the associated invoice and shipping documents.

○ Exporters should submit shipping documents along with declaration forms duly signed by customs within 21 days from the date of exports.

SHIPPING TERMS

The following are more terms relating to shipping:

bill of lading, C & F, CIF, FOB destination, FOB shipping point

---

short-term /ʃɔrt tɜrm/

BASIC

ADJECTIVE Something that is **short-term** has continued for less than a year or will continue for less than a year.

○ The Fund is keeping maturities short because short-term investments are currently the highest-yielding segment of the market.

○ *The higher interest on short-term borrowings may have caused interest expenses to rise during the year.*

▶ **SYNONYM:**
current

---

sin|gle en|try /sɪŋᵊl ɛntri/

BASIC

NOUN **Single entry** is a bookkeeping system in which all transactions are entered in one account only, as in a check register.

○ *It is likely that the company would enter details of a transaction once only, using a single entry accounting system.*

○ *Single entry accounting is a simple bookkeeping system in which transactions are recorded in a single record.*

> **RELATED WORDS**
>
> Compare this with **double entry** bookkeeping, in which all transactions are entered in two places, as a debit in one account and as a credit in another.

---

stand|ard cost /stændərd kɔst/ (**standard costs**)

MANAGEMENT

NOUN A **standard cost** is the budgeted cost of a regular manufacturing process against which actual costs are compared.

○ *Of course, if a new product, service, or process is to be carried out, the initial standard costs will have to be estimated.*

○ *Factory variance is the difference between product transferred at standard cost, and production at actual cost.*

---

state|ment /steɪtmənt/ (**statements**)

COMMERCE

NOUN A **statement** is a printed document containing a summary of bills or invoices and displaying the total amount due.

○ *At the end of each billing cycle you will receive a statement.*

○ *Transactions and interest payments are recorded in a monthly statement or in a small book held by the owner of the account.*

---

state|ment of cash flows (ABBR SCF) /steɪtmənt əv kæʃ floʊz/ (statements of cash flows)

NOUN A **statement of cash flows** is a financial statement that shows the amounts of cash that came into and went out of a company over a particular period of time.

○ *By using a statement of cash flows, managers can plan and manage their cash sources and needs from different types of business activities.*

○ *Whatever the sources and uses of cash, the statement of cash flows tells a great deal about a business's health.*

---

state|ment of earn|ings and com|pre|hen|sive in|come /steɪtmənt əv ɜrnɪŋz ənd kɒmprɪhɛnsɪv ɪnkʌm/ (statements of earnings and comprehensive income)

NOUN A **statement of earnings and comprehensive income** is a single financial statement that contains all items of income and expense for a particular accounting period.

○ *The Financial Accounting Standards Board requires a single statement of earnings and comprehensive income and requires a subtotal for net income.*

○ *The statement of earnings and comprehensive income measures profitability of the company by showing the income earned and expenses incurred during a particular accounting period.*

---

stock¹ /stɒk/

NOUN A company's **stock** is the total number of its shares.

○ *Two years later, when the company went public, their stock was valued at $38 million.*

○ *She works for a bank, buying and selling stocks.*

TALKING ABOUT STOCK

We say that stock is **trading at** a particular price.

If analysts say how much a stock is worth, they **value** it. If they set the amount too low, they **undervalue** it.

If analysts **downgrade** stock, they change its rating in a negative way, for instance from "buy" to "sell."

---

stock² /stɒk/

MANAGEMENT

NOUN A store's **stock** is the goods that it has available to sell.

○ That buyer ordered $27,500 worth of stock.

○ Most of the store's stock was destroyed in the fire.

▶ **SYNONYM:**
inventory

---

straight-line de|pre|ci|a|tion /streɪt laɪn dɪpriːʃieɪʃən/

TAX

NOUN **Straight-line depreciation** is a method of depreciation in which an equal amount of depreciation is taken each year.

○ The straight-line depreciation method is the most popular method when a company has no need to recognize depreciation costs at an accelerated rate.

○ Straight-line depreciation is calculated by subtracting an asset's expected salvage value from its capitalized cost.

---

sub|con|tract /sʌbkɒntrækt/ (subcontracts, subcontracted, subcontracting)

BASIC

VERB If one company **subcontracts** part of its work **to** another company, it pays the other company to do part of the work that it has been employed to do.

○ The company is subcontracting production of most of the parts.

○ Specialist machining work was subcontracted by the company to a total of 120 suppliers scattered around the country.

> **WORD BUILDER**
>
> **sub-** = less important, or a smaller part
>
> The prefix **sub-** often appears in words connected with something that is a smaller part of another thing, or with words to do with passing on a responsibility, debt, etc. to someone else: **subcontract**, **sublease**, **subsidiary**.

---

sub|lease /sʌblis/ (subleases)

BASIC

NOUN A **sublease** is the lease of all or part of a rented property by a tenant to a third person.

○ Normally, the nature of a sublease agreement does not affect the original lease agreement, and the original lessee retains primary liability.

○ The sublease payments were recorded as reductions of monthly rent expense.

---

sub|sid|i|ar|y /səbsɪdiɛri/ (subsidiaries)

BASIC

NOUN A **subsidiary** is a company that is part of a larger and more important company.

○ WM Financial Services is a subsidiary of Washington Mutual.

○ They are considering raising part of their future capital requirements by forming new subsidiaries and selling a portion of their equity to the public.

---

sunk cost /sʌŋk kɔst/ (sunk costs)

MANAGEMENT

NOUN A **sunk cost** is an expense that you have already paid for or committed to and which you cannot change.

○ The sunk cost is the money that cannot be recovered by subsequent resale of an asset.

○ Your investment is a sunk cost to you; the firm does not have to pay you, after the fact, for the specific investment.

sup|pli|er /səplaɪər/ (suppliers)

COMMERCE

NOUN A company's **suppliers** are businesses that supply the company with products or materials.

○ *The company does not make its own products, and thus has no control over manufacturing by its suppliers, who are based in Asia and Europe.*

○ *Some foreign suppliers of raw materials won't release goods until they receive cash payment or a letter of credit from the bank.*

WORD BUILDER

-er = person that does something

The suffix **-er** often appears in words for people or organizations that do a particular thing: **customer**, **receiver**, **shareholder**, **supplier**.

---

sup|ply chain /səplaɪ tʃeɪn/

MANAGEMENT

NOUN The **supply chain** is all of the various stages, in order, of a product's progress from raw materials through production and distribution of the finished product, until it reaches the consumer.

○ *Lean manufacturing processes aim to eliminate waste across the supply chain.*

○ *These changes will benefit many companies looking for a shortened supply chain and increased efficiency.*

sur|plus¹ /sɜrplʌs/ (surpluses)

BASIC

NOUN A **surplus** is an excess of total assets over total liabilities.

○ *The trade surplus is likely to persist, and reserve assets, after all, are generating interest incomes.*

○ *A pension fund has a surplus when its assets exceed its obligations to current and future pensioners.*

RELATED WORDS

The opposite of **surplus** is **deficit**, for both its senses.

---

sur|plus² /sˈɜrplʌs/ (surpluses)

BASIC

NOUN A **surplus** is an excess of revenue over expenditure during a particular accounting period.

○ A charity's surplus at the end of a financial year is not liable to taxation.

○ Not-for-profit institutions treat a surplus of operating revenues over operating costs as a profit that they are not supposed to make.

sus|pense ac|count /səspˈɛns əkaʊnt/ (suspense accounts)

FINANCIAL STATEMENTS

NOUN A **suspense account** is a temporary account in which entries are made until a permanent decision is made about where the entries should go.

○ This account is a suspense account for unallocated payments.

○ The use of the suspense account allows a set of accounts to be prepared subject to the correction of the errors.

S

Tt

T ac|count /ti əkaʊnt/ (T accounts)

BASIC

NOUN A **T account** is a type of account that uses two columns to show debits and credits.

○ After all transactions are posted to the T account, the amounts on each side are totaled.

○ The disadvantage of the T account is that it requires totaling the debit and the credit columns in order to find the balance.

tan|gi|ble /tændʒɪbᵊl/

BASIC

ADJECTIVE A business asset that is **tangible** is a physical asset, such as a factory or office.

○ Capital, in the form of tangible assets such as machinery or intangible assets such as money, can be a key consideration.

○ Tangible assets include a company's physical property like real estate, factories, equipment, and inventories as well as its financial balances.

tax /tæks/ (taxes)

TAX

COUNT/NONCOUNT NOUN **Tax** is an amount of money that you have to pay to the government so that it can pay for public services such as roads and schools.

○ The government has pledged not to raise taxes on people below a certain income.

○ Cutting capital gains tax would leave some people paying less tax than other people with the same income.

TALKING ABOUT TAX

If a government makes you pay tax, they **levy** or **impose** a tax.

If you take tax off an amount, you **deduct** it, and if you claim back tax you have already paid, you **reclaim** it.

Some costs can be **offset against** tax, which means that you pay less tax because of them.

If someone tries to **evade** or **avoid** tax, they try to find ways not to pay it. If you do not have to pay tax on something, that thing is tax **exempt**.

---

tax|a|ble /tˈæksəbᵊl/

TAX

ADJECTIVE **Taxable** income is income on which you have to pay tax.

○ It is worth consulting the guide to see whether your income is taxable.

○ Deductions can only be used to reduce taxable income, so their value depends on each taxpayer's tax bracket.

---

tax|a|tion /tækseɪʃᵊn/

TAX

NOUN **Taxation** is the system by which a government takes money from people and organizations and spends it on things such as education, health, and defense.

○ The plan would allow individuals to exclude from taxation 30 percent of their gain from the sale or exchange of long-held assets.

○ Individuals can exclude from taxation 30 percent of their gain from the sale or exchange of a variety of assets held for more than a year.

---

tax a|void|ance /tæks əvɔɪdəns/

TAX

NOUN **Tax avoidance** is the act of finding lawful ways of reducing the amount of tax that you have to pay.

○ Tax avoidance can be achieved by taking maximum advantage of taxation allowances and reliefs.

○ *Self-employed people have more scope for tax avoidance than people working for someone else, and they often enjoy legitimate tax breaks denied to wage and salary earners.*

WHICH WORD
Tax avoidance or tax evasion?

Tax avoidance refers to legal methods of reducing tax payments, while **tax evasion** refers to illegal methods of reducing tax payments.

---

tax de|duct|i|ble /tæks dɪdʌktɪbᵊl/

Tax

ADJECTIVE If an expense or loss is **tax deductible**, it can be paid out of the part of your income on which you do not pay tax, so that the amount of tax that you pay is reduced.

○ *The interest is tax deductible, so the interest cost is less than the tax-free gain on the house price.*

○ *Tax policy has also encouraged employee contributions to pension funds by making them tax deductible.*

---

tax de|duc|tion /tæks dɪdʌkʃᵊn/ (tax deductions)

Tax

NOUN A **tax deduction** is an expense that may be deducted for tax purposes.

○ *Currently, businesses get a tax deduction of as much as $35,000 for architectural changes designed to aid customers or employees with disabilities.*

○ *For a contribution to a charitable organization to produce a tax deduction, the donor must rid himself of all control over the property given.*

---

tax-de|ferred /tæks dɪfɜrd/

Tax

ADJECTIVE If an income or account is **tax-deferred**, it will be taxed in a later accounting period.

○ *If your retirement plan includes both taxable and tax-deferred accounts, it is worth considering which funds should be placed in each.*

○ *Most fixed annuities have a minimum rate, typically 3 percent, and your earnings are tax-deferred until you withdraw them.*

tax de|pre|ci|a|tion /tæks dɪprɪʃieɪʲªn/

TAX

NOUN **Tax depreciation** is depreciation in a company's internal financial records that is different from the amount that is used for the internal books.

- ○ *Tax depreciation is taken as an expense on your tax return each year for whatever depreciable assets you have.*
- ○ *Tax depreciation deductions are greater than book depreciation expense amounts early in the life of a depreciable asset, but that situation reverses in later years.*

tax e|va|sion /tæks əveɪʒªn/

TAX

NOUN **Tax evasion** is the act of reducing the amount of tax that you have to pay by using illegal methods.

- ○ *The former director of the company pleaded guilty last year to criminal charges of money laundering, insider trading, and income tax evasion.*
- ○ *High rates of tax encourage tax evasion, and discourage hard work and the taking of risks.*

tax ex|empt¹ /tæks ɪgzɛmpt/

TAX

ADJECTIVE If an income or property is **tax exempt**, you do not have to pay tax on it.

- ○ *Because the interest income from some bonds may be tax exempt, the housing authority pays a low interest rate to bondholders.*
- ○ *Probably the most efficient tax system of all is an expenditure tax, under which all savings would be tax exempt.*

tax ex|empt² /tæks ɪgzɛmpt/

TAX

ADJECTIVE If an asset is **tax exempt**, it is earning income that is not subject to taxation.

- ○ *There is a statutory rule in the US that denies a deduction for expenses incurred in connection with tax-exempt income.*
- ○ *The increase in interest income is primarily the result of changing the Company's investment portfolio from tax exempt securities to taxable securities.*

t

tax loss /tæks lɔs/ (**tax losses**)

TAX

NOUN A **tax loss** is a loss made by a company that can be set against future tax payments.

○ Firms with large accumulated tax loss carry-forwards shouldn't borrow at all.

○ There are current moves to establish withholding taxes on portfolio holdings in major financial centers in order to reduce the tax loss on the profits generated there.

tax rate /tæks reɪt/ (**tax rates**)

TAX

NOUN The **tax rate** is the percentage of an income or an amount of money that has to be paid as tax.

○ These officials prefer lower tax rates on capital gains.

○ The budget may bring down the corporate tax rate from 35 percent to 30 percent, the peak rate of individual tax.

tax re|fund /tæks rifʌnd/ (**tax refunds**)

TAX

NOUN A **tax refund** is money received back from a tax return.

○ By recording Gift Aid donations on their tax returns, higher-rated taxpayers can receive a further 18 percent tax refund.

○ The additional payments will result in either a larger tax refund or a smaller tax bill at the end of the year.

tax re|lief /tæks rəlif/

TAX

NOUN **Tax relief** is a reduction in the amount of tax that a person or company has to pay.

○ Both employer and employee can claim tax relief on the contributions that they make to the scheme.

○ Among the biggest beneficiaries of tax relief on investments are the charitable trusts.

tax re|turn /tæks rɪtɜrn/ (**tax returns**)

TAX

NOUN A **tax return** is an official form that you fill in with details about your income so that the tax that you owe can be calculated.

○ Each shareholder reports his proportionate share of the loss on his tax return.

○ People complete an annual tax return which shows all receipts and all savings.

tax year /tæks yɪər/

TAX

NOUN A **tax year** is a period of twelve months which is used by the government as a basis for calculating taxes.

○ Foreign income will be translated into US dollars at the average exchange rate for the tax year in which the transactions are conducted.

○ The payments on account are based on the income for the previous tax year.

tem|po|rar|y ac|count /tɛmpəreri əkaunt/ (**temporary accounts**)

FINANCIAL STATEMENTS: INCOME STATEMENT

NOUN A **temporary account** is an account which is closed out at the end of the year.

○ The temporary account balances must be reduced to zero at the end of each fiscal period.

○ Most businesses close the revenues and expenses to another temporary account used solely in the closing process.

terms of pay|ment /tɜrmz əv peɪmənt/

COMMERCE

NOUN The **terms of payment** of a sale state how and when an invoice is to be paid.

○ The terms of payment were 50 percent down and 50 percent on completion.

○ The leading auctioneers offer inducements such as guaranteed prices to persuade sellers to part with their treasures, and generous terms of payment for buyers.

t

trade dis|count /treɪd dɪskaʊnt/ (trade discounts)

COMMERCE

NOUN A **trade discount** is an amount by which the price of something is reduced for a person or business in the same trade.

○ *People in the building trade can get trade discounts of up to 50 percent.*

○ *We have a number of tradesmen who, although too small to buy directly from the wholesalers, purchase from us at a trade discount.*

trans|ac|tion /trænzækʃᵊn/ (transactions)

BASIC

NOUN A **transaction** is a piece of business that changes the finances of a company, for example an act of buying or selling something.

○ *The transaction is completed by payment of the fee.*

○ *The data management system tracks the complete record of every transaction with a customer from the point that their name is entered in its order books.*

trans|fer pric|ing /trænsfɜr praɪsɪŋ/

MANAGEMENT

NOUN **Transfer pricing** is the setting of a price for the transfer of materials, goods, or services between different parts of a large organization.

○ *He claims that foreign companies are engaged in massive tax avoidance through transfer pricing.*

○ *Setting prices for the transfer of products between the departments is known as transfer pricing.*

trans|la|tion /trænzleɪʃᵊn/

BASIC

NOUN **Translation** is the act of converting one currency into another.

○ *Revenues and earnings remain under pressure from the negative impact of translation of international currencies into a stronger US dollar.*

○ *Translation is the process whereby financial data denominated in one currency are expressed in terms of another currency.*

WORD BUILDER
-ation = action

The suffix **-ation** often appears in nouns that relate to the action of the verb they are formed from: **allocation**, **amortization**, **capitalization**, **diversification**, **modification**, **reconciliation**, **taxation**, **translation**, **valuation**.

---

trans|pose /trænspoʊz/ (transposes, transposed, transposing)

BASIC

VERB If you **transpose** two numbers, you make an error in which the order of the numbers is reversed.

○ He had inadvertently transposed two numbers in the previous year's inventory balance, resulting in a material understatement of the previous year's ending inventory.

○ The accountant discovered that two digits had been transposed, recording $520 as $250.

---

tri|al bal|ance /traɪəl bæləns/ (trial balances)

FINANCIAL STATEMENTS

NOUN A **trial balance** is a statement of all the credits and debits in a double entry accounting system, created in order to test that they are equal.

○ The trial balance consists of taking and listing every balance in the ledger at that date in order to carry out an arithmetic check of the double entry system.

○ To test that the total of debits and credits in the accounts are equal, the accountant periodically prepares a trial balance.

---

turn|o|ver /tɜrnoʊvər/

MANAGEMENT

NOUN A company's **turnover** is the value of the goods or services that it sells during a particular period of time, usually a year.

○ The company had a turnover of $3.8 million.

○ They expect 25 percent of their annual turnover next year to come from exports.

t

Uu

un|al|lo|cat|ed /ʌnˈæləkeɪtɪd/

BASIC

ADJECTIVE **Unallocated** amounts or costs are not associated with any particular activity.

○ A substantial amount of previously unallocated equity was allocated back to members of the cooperatives.

○ While some of the tax benefits were due to net losses, seven cooperatives received a benefit by allocating unallocated equity back to members.

> **WORD BUILDER**
> **un-** = not
>
> The prefix **un-** is often added to adjectives to make their opposites: **unallocated**, **unbalanced**, **unrestricted**, **unsecured**.

un|ap|pro|pri|at|ed /ʌnəˈproʊprieɪtɪd/

BASIC

ADJECTIVE **Unappropriated** funds are funds that have not been intended for any particular purpose.

○ Where the subsidiary has unappropriated profits at the beginning of the year, these will be either pre-acquisition profits or profits earned since acquisition and not distributed.

○ Unappropriated retained earnings are the part of a company's profits not distributed as dividends or set aside for a particular use.

U

149 | **unrealized gains**

un|bal|anced /ʌnbælənst/

FINANCIAL STATEMENTS

ADJECTIVE If an account is **unbalanced**, its total debit balances are not equal to total credit balances.

○ In practice, most governments run unbalanced budgets as a means of regulating the level of economic activity.

○ Most computerized accounting packages prevent one-sided and unbalanced journal entries from being recorded.

un|der|stat|ed /ʌndərsteɪtɪd/

FINANCIAL STATEMENTS

ADJECTIVE If an account or a figure on an account is **understated**, the amount that is reported on the financial statement is less than it should be.

○ If a loan that ought to have been reported is kept off the books, liabilities will be understated.

○ Accounts payable were understated by approximately $20 million that year.

un|earned in|come /ʌnɜrnd ɪnkʌm/

FINANCIAL STATEMENTS: BALANCE SHEET

NOUN **Unearned income** is income that is received before it is earned by goods being delivered or services performed, or income that you do not have to work to earn, such as from property and investment.

○ In Britain all the self-employed earners, taken together, generate less income than that made from dividend payments and similar unearned income such as rent.

○ Unearned income is cash received in advance of earning income.

un|re|al|ized gains /ʌnrɪəlaɪzd geɪnz/

FINANCIAL STATEMENTS: INCOME STATEMENT

NOUN **Unrealized gains** are gains from the increase in value of an asset that you still own.

○ The funds can rid themselves of capital gains inherent in the fund by transferring out the securities with the highest unrealized gains.

○ Because increases in value generally arise through the holding of assets rather than trading or operating activities, they tend to be labeled unrealized gains and are separated from other income.

un|re|al|ized loss|es /ʌnriəlaɪzd lɔsɪz/

FINANCIAL STATEMENTS: INCOME STATEMENT

NOUN **Unrealized losses** are losses from the decrease in value of an asset that you still own.

○ Public companies must ensure that they have provided for unrealized losses before calculating profits available for distribution.

○ Unrealized losses are recorded to the profit and loss account when market price falls below average acquisition cost.

un|re|strict|ed /ʌnrɪstrɪktɪd/

BASIC

ADJECTIVE **Unrestricted** money is money that can be used for any purpose.

○ Working funds are unrestricted funds derived from rates and charges revenue, and are invested as a form of savings against unforeseen expenses.

○ Unrestricted contributions are those contributions that are free of donor restrictions on their usage.

un|se|cured /ʌnsɪkyʊərd/

INVESTING

ADJECTIVE An **unsecured** loan or debt is not guaranteed by an asset such as a person's home.

○ The group's total debts include $900 million in unsecured loans and an additional $700 million that is secured against specific assets.

○ Two scandals involving local banks whose managements had lent millions of dollars in unsecured loans have sapped public confidence.

U

Vv

---

val|u|a|tion /ˈvælyueɪʃən/ (valuations)

BASIC

COUNT/NONCOUNT NOUN A **valuation** is a judgment that someone makes about how much something is worth.

- ○ The company said that the total purchase price is slightly below the low end of its valuation of these assets.
- ○ If the market valuation of the subsidiary does increase, the gains should, at a later date, spill over to the shareholder.

---

val|ue /ˈvælyu/ (values)

BASIC

NOUN The **value** of something is how much money it is worth.

- ○ The value of his investment rose by $50,000 in a year.
- ○ Around 1m elderly homeowners have at least $100,000 locked up in the value of their houses.

---

val|ue add|ed /ˈvælyu ˈædɪd/

MANAGEMENT

NOUN **Value added** is the difference between the cost of goods purchased by a business and its revenue.

- ○ Sales volume is less important than value added.
- ○ The ranking is based on market value added, which is the difference between the capital invested in a company and its market valuation.

var|i|a|ble costs /vɛəriəbᵊl kɔsts/
MANAGEMENT

NOUN **Variable costs** are costs that vary depending on how much of
a product is made.

○ We managed to reduce our expenses by controlling the variable costs such
as raw materials and fuel consumption.

○ Power and coal alone can add up to 40 percent of the variable costs in
a cement plant.

▶ SYNONYM:
direct costs

var|i|ance /vɛəriəns/ (variances)
MANAGEMENT

COUNT/NONCOUNT NOUN **Variance** is the difference between an actual
cost and a budgeted or standard cost.

○ The purpose of variance analysis is to provide practical pointers to the causes
of off-standard performance so that management can improve operations.

○ Favorable or positive variances occur when revenue is higher, or cost lower,
than anticipated or planned, leading to a better profit result.

ven|dor /vɛndər/ (vendors)
COMMERCE

NOUN A **vendor** is a company or person that sells a product or service.

○ The company is struggling with inventory shortages, and faces more
problems ahead as vendors say they will supply new merchandise only on
a cash basis.

○ The company has reduced production costs by following strategies like the
global sourcing of components and reducing the number of direct vendors
with which it interacts.

V

void /vɔɪd/
COMMERCE

VERB If you **void** a check or an invoice, you cancel it by changing the
amount to zero, while leaving the transaction still posted.

○ Items that are sequentially numbered such as checks, invoices, and purchase orders are voided rather than deleted so that every numbered document can be accounted for.

○ When you void an invoice, the invoice number continues to exist so that you can account for it.

---

vouch|er /vˈaʊtʃər/ (vouchers)

COMMERCE

NOUN A **voucher** is a document showing payment information, or a document that can be presented to receive money.

○ The scheme will give vouchers to cover the cost of private treatment if waiting lists are too long.

○ Cash welfare benefits were replaced with vouchers for food and other essentials.

V

Ww

---

wag|es /weɪdʒɪz/

`BASIC`

NOUN Someone's **wages** are the amount of money that is regularly paid to them for the work that they do.

○ Women's average hourly wages are 22 percent lower than men's.

○ Economists warned that dangers of pressure for higher wages could lead to an even greater jump in inflation.

---

ware|house /weərhaʊs/ (warehouses)

`COMMERCE`

NOUN A **warehouse** is a large building where goods are stored before they are sold.

○ A pile-up of unsold goods in stores and warehouses is a sign that production is outstripping demand.

○ Goods were continuously delivered to the company's warehouses, from where they were selected, re-packed, and dispatched to retail stores.

---

ware|house re|ceipt /weərhaʊs rɪsit/ (warehouse receipts)

`COMMERCE`

NOUN A **warehouse receipt** is a document that shows proof of ownership of goods that are stored in a warehouse.

○ If you place goods in a public warehouse, the warehouse company gives you a warehouse receipt and will then release the goods only on the instructions of the holder of the receipt.

○ A warehouse receipt is a document that provides proof of ownership of commodities that are stored in a warehouse, vault, or depository for safekeeping.

weight|ed av|er|age cost of cap|i|tal (ABBR **WACC**)
/weɪtɪd ævərɪdʒ kɒst əv kæpɪtəl/

MANAGEMENT

NOUN The **weighted average cost of capital** is the cost of capital that is adjusted according to the percentages of debt financing and equity financing.

○ *The weighted average cost of capital takes into account both debt and equity sources of capital.*

○ *The weighted average cost of capital is the percentage rate of return that must be achieved to add shareholder value taking into account all the various sources of finance used by the firm.*

---

whole|sale /hoʊlseɪl/

COMMERCE

ADJECTIVE A **wholesale** business is a business that sells in large quantities to another business that will resell the items or use them for manufacturing.

○ *The company decided to press its suppliers for lower prices and to pass on any wholesale price increases to its customers.*

○ *Within ten years they had built a large and highly profitable wholesale business, selling to the industrial users of electronic equipment.*

▶ **COLLOCATIONS:**
wholesale business
wholesale price

---

wire trans|fer /waɪər trænsfər/ (**wire transfers**)

COMMERCE

NOUN A **wire transfer** is a direct payment of money from one bank account into another.

○ *The fastest but most expensive arrangement for transferring funds is wire transfer, and a slower but cheaper method is a depository transfer check.*

○ *Can you stop payment on an electronic wire transfer in the same way as you can with checks?*

W

with|draw /wɪðˈdrɔ/ (withdraws, withdrew, withdrawn, withdrawing)

COMMERCE

VERB If you **withdraw** money **from** a bank account, you take it out of that account.

○ *Savers are withdrawing money and then redepositing it in order to claim the higher rate.*

○ *Deposit outflows occur when depositors withdraw cash from checking or savings accounts or write checks that are deposited in other banks.*

work|ing cap|i|tal /wɜrkɪŋ kæpɪtəl/

MANAGEMENT

NOUN **Working capital** is money that is available for use immediately, rather than money invested in land or equipment.

○ *Funds for the buyback will come from working capital and bank borrowings.*

○ *The project has been put on hold for lack of working capital.*

work-in-pro|gress (ABBR **WIP**) /wɜrk ɪn prɒgrɛs/

MANAGEMENT

NOUN **Work-in-progress** is the value of work that has begun but which has not been completed, as shown in a profit and loss account.

○ *Adopting regular billing to reduce work-in-progress is likely to improve cash flow.*

○ *The company has generated 2 million cash from improved control of stocks and work-in-progress.*

write down /raɪt daʊn/ (writes down, wrote down, written down, writing down)

FINANCIAL STATEMENTS

VERB If you **write down** an asset, you decrease its book value.

○ *For the next several quarters regulators will be writing down assets and selling off perhaps 500 other insolvent funds.*

○ *The group may have to write down the value of some of its overseas investments.*

W

▶ **COLLOCATION:**
write down a value

---

write off /raɪt ɒf/ (**writes off, wrote off, written off, writing off**)

FINANCIAL STATEMENTS: BALANCE SHEET

VERB If you **write off** a bad debt or obsolete asset, you cancel it from the accounts.

○ In some cases customers will not pay money owed and the accounts receivable must be written off to bad debt expense.

○ The business will write off this bad debt by reducing the number of debtors on its balance sheet and reducing the amount of profit on its profit-and-loss accounts.

▶ **COLLOCATION:**
write off a debt

---

write-off /raɪt ɒf/

FINANCIAL STATEMENTS: BALANCE SHEET

NOUN A **write-off** is an amount corresponding to the book value of the bad debt or obsolete asset that is canceled from an account against gross profits.

○ The bulk of the write-off by the company is related to bottling operations, advertising, and marketing.

○ A write-off of an asset may take the form of depreciation (or cost recovery), depletion, or amortization.

---

write-up /raɪt ʌp/

FINANCIAL STATEMENTS

NOUN A **write-up** is the act of doing the trial balance and financial statements at the end of the year.

○ Essentially, the write-up is only concerned with creating a trial balance, usually just to do the taxes.

○ She does write-up work for clients, recording their accounting transactions in accounting records, and preparing their financial statements.

w

year end (ABBR **YE**) /yɪər ɛnd/

BASIC

NOUN The **year end** is the date when a business's fiscal year ends, or the accounting work done at this time.

○ *The company plans to sell the rights that it owns by year end and use the proceeds to pay off its creditors.*

○ *The transaction is subject to regulatory approval and is expected to be completed by year end.*

yield /yiːld/ (**yields**)

BASIC

NOUN The **yield** of an investment is the amount of money or profit that it produces.

○ *The high yields available on the dividend shares made them attractive to private investors.*

○ *Real estate prices are low, but the rental market is likely to produce better yields.*

Practice and Solutions

1. For each question, choose the correct answer.

1 The hours of a service for which you have to pay are described as
   ....
   a negotiable   **b** billable   **c** cumulative

2 Dividends or earnings that can be added from period to period are
   ....
   a cumulative   **b** tangible   **c** unallocated

3 Money that can be used for any purpose is ....
   a retroactive   **b** unrestricted   **c** negotiable

4 A loan or creditor that has an asset pledged as collateral to be taken if
   the debt is not repaid is ....
   a material   **b** insolvent   **c** secured

5 If something you use for your business loses value and will therefore
   count toward reducing your tax, it is ....
   a billable   **b** residual   **c** depreciable

6 Physical assets such as a factory or office are ....
   a tangible   **b** material   **c** wholesale

2. Match the two parts together.

1 If you bring forward an amount,

2 If you close out an account,

3 If you write down an asset,

4 If you carry forward a loss or credit,

5 If you gross up income or wages,

6 If you write off a bad debt,

a you increase them to their value before tax or deductions.

b you cancel it from the accounts.

c you apply it to the following tax year.

d you terminate it, usually by selling securities.

e you move it to the next page or column.

f you decrease its book value.

3. Match the two parts together.

1 If you accrue an expense or income,

2 If you transpose two numbers,

3 If you withdraw money from a bank account,

4 If you reimburse someone for something,

5 If a person or organization defaults on a payment,

6 If you allocate funds,

a they fail to pay an amount that they owe.

b you pay them back the money that they have spent or lost because of it.

c you recognize it before it has been paid or been received.

d you divide up or distribute them.

e you take it out of that account.

f you make an error in which the order of the numbers is reversed.

4. Choose the correct word to fill each gap.

rotten	sick	bad

1 A .... debt is a sum of money that a person or company owes but is not likely to pay back.

prime	sunk	majority

2 A .... cost is the part of the cost of a commodity that changes according to the amount of it that is produced, such as materials and labor.

efficient	exempt	zero

3 If an income or property is tax ...., you do not have to pay tax on it.

prepaid	minus	depreciation

4 A .... expense is the amount deducted from gross profit to allow for a reduction in the value of something because of its age or how much it has been used.

Working	Agent	Secured

5 .... capital is money that is available for use immediately, rather than money invested in land or equipment.

additional	incoming	accrual

6 An .... basis is a system of accounting where income is recognized before payment is received and expenses are recognized before they are paid.

5. Rearrange the letters to find words. Use the definitions to help you.

1 **diiuqlity**   ....
   (A company's ability to turn its assets into cash.)

2 **ecablan**   ....
   (The net amount in an account at a particular time, including all credits and debits.)

3 **ernrvout**   ....
   (The value of the goods or services that a company sells during a particular period of time, usually a year.)

4 **tepyt chsa**   ....
   (Money that is kept in the office of a company, for making small payments in cash when necessary.)

5 **aaptcil**   ....
   (Money that you use to start a business.)

6 **daehvore**   ....
   (The regular and essential expenses of running a business, such as salaries, rent, and bills.)

6. Complete the sentences by writing one word in each gap.

lessee	lessor	auditor
creditor	vendor	payee

1 An .... is an accountant who officially examines the accounts of organizations.

2 A .... is a person who is paying to lease an asset such as a car or building.

3 A .... is a company or person that sells a product or service.

4 A .... is a person who is to receive money.

5 A .... is an organization or person that people owe money to.

6 A .... is the owner of an asset such as a car or building, who is renting it out to the lessee.

7. Match the two parts together.

1 A warehouse receipt is a document

a containing full details of goods that are being transported by ship.

2 A bank statement is a document

b issued by a seller to a buyer that lists the goods or services that have been supplied and says how much money the buyer owes for them.

3 An invoice is a document

4 A bill of lading is a document

c sent by a seller to a purchaser that includes full details of the transaction.

5 A remittance advice is a document

d that shows proof of ownership of goods that are stored in a warehouse.

6 A bill of sale is a document

e showing all the money paid into and taken out of a bank account during a particular period of time.

f that describes payments that are being made, especially the part of the invoice that the customer sends back with payment.

8. Find the words or phrases that do not belong.

1 Types of account ....
a asset account **b** merchant account **c** bankrupt account
d equity account

2 Types of profit ....
a liquid profit **b** operating profit **c** gross profit **d** net profit

3 Types of loss ....
a loss on translation **b** ordinary loss **c** loss on broking **d** tax loss

4 Documents ....
a annual report **b** allocation **c** balanced scorecard **d** bill of lading

5 Types of stock ....
a preferred stock **b** capital stock **c** common stock
d uncommon stock

6 Types of assets ....
a current assets **b** liquid assets **c** hanging assets **d** fixed assets

9. Complete the sentences by writing one word in each gap.

reimbursed	capitalized	accrued
budgeted	debited	defaulted

1 She had been experiencing financial difficulties and had
.... on several large loans.

2 We have .... $16,000 for maintenance of the
building.

3   The remaining amount will be .... from your
account on May 10th.

4   The company .... him for the expenses he had
incurred.

5   You will have to pay any interest that has ....
in that period.

6   We were lucky enough to find two enthusiastic backers who
.... the business.

10. Complete the sentences by writing a word or phrase in each gap.

cost center	allocation	audit
opportunity cost	bookkeeping	revenue stream

1   We have made an .... of $15,000 for the
campaign committee.

2   My accountant prepares our financial reports, but I do all the
.... myself.

3   We need to calculate the .... of tying up such
a large sum of money.

4   The human resources department is the company's biggest .
....

5   Consulting provides our firm with its most consistent
....

6   We have appointed a different firm to carry out this year's
....

11. Choose the correct word or phrase to fill each gap.

---

a deferred   an advance   a previous

---

1 We had to make .... payment to cover the cost of the materials.

---

referral   deficit   refund

---

2 The government has cut public spending in order to reduce the
....

---

performance   operating   proceeding

---

3 My department has an annual .... budget of $1.3 million.

---

reclassify   allocate   reconcile

---

4 It is important to .... the account at the end of each quarter.

---

portable   fluid   liquid

---

5 We were able to raise enough cash by selling off some of the company's
.... assets.

---

close   end   finish

---

6 In order to .... the books, our accountants need all the relevant documentation.

12. Put each sentence into the correct order.

1 we were unable / of working capital / of our lack / to open another / branch because

   ....

   ....

2 is their / that the code / intellectual property / for the software / they insist

   ....

   ....

3 within ten months / to reach / breakeven point / we expect / on the product

   ....

   ....

4 for small purchases / petty cash / we use / stamps and coffee / such as

   ....

   ....

5 was able to / the organization / its reserves / fund the new building / out of

   ....

   ....

6 of directors / there is / in the company's / a full list / annual report

   ....

   ....

13. Which sentences are correct?

1 All our forecasts are adjusted of inflation. ....

2 We were shocked to discover that we had been billed .... for their time.

3 For tax purposes, he is classified as a sole trader. ....

4 The full amount was credited in your account last month. ....

5 What do you do if someone defaults on a payment? ....

6 They subcontracted the IT on an offshore company. ....

14. Rearrange the letters to find words. Use the definitions to help you.

1 **unbos** ....
(An extra amount of money that is paid to shareholders out of profits, or that is given to employees.)

2 **eageervl** ....
(The amount of borrowed money that a company uses to run its business.)

3 **dahsrlrehoe** ....
(An investor who owns one or more shares of stock in a company.)

4 **idnesdivd** ....
(The part of a company's profits that is paid out to the shareholders.)

5 **qtiyeu** ....
(The sum of your assets or investments once your debts have been subtracted.)

6 **oocripranot** ....

(A large business or company.)

15. Put each sentence into the correct order.

1 to secure the loan / their home / they used / as collateral /
they needed

....

....

2 to buy / the land sale / the proceeds of / we used / a refrigeration unit

....

....

3 from Scandinavia / imported / the raw materials / are mainly /
that we use

....

....

4 be prepared / I asked him / a cash discount / if he would / to offer

....

....

5 increased profitability / for our business / production methods /
have led to / more efficient

....

....

6 rate of return / investments can / a higher / more risky /
potentially deliver

....

....

16. Rearrange the letters to find words. Use the definitions to help you.

1 **cytbkrpuna** ....
(A legal recognition that a person, organization, or company does not have sufficient assets to repay its debts.)

2 **ecniiov** ....
(A document issued by a seller to a buyer that lists the goods or services that have been supplied and says how much money the buyer owes for them.)

3 **erecpit** ....
(A written statement that shows that you have received goods or money.)

4 **seouherwa** ....
(A large building where goods are stored before they are sold.)

5 **remchadnesi** ....
(Products that are bought, sold, or traded.)

6 **ificedt** ....
(A situation in which liabilities are greater than assets.)

17. Complete the sentences by writing one word in each gap.

value	loss	year
account	rates	tax

1 In this country, people who earn a lot pay a higher amount of income ....

2 We get very little income from our savings, because interest .... are low at the moment.

3 I decided to put that money into a savings ....
   for my children.

4 There are still some large bills to pay before the end of the financial
   ....

5 This bill has a face .... of $50.

6 Our finance director has prepared a profit and
   .... statement.

18. For each question, choose the correct answer.

a collateral	a deficit	a deferral

1 A transaction that will be recognized in a later accounting period is
   ....

personal property	preferred stock	shareholders' equity

2 The shares in a company that are owned by people who have the right
   to receive part of the company's profits before the holders of common
   stock are ....

gross profit	net profit	net loss

3 The difference between a company's total income from sales and its
   total production costs is its ....

a lockbox	a chargeback	a cash book

4 A bank account set up to receive payments from customers is
   ....

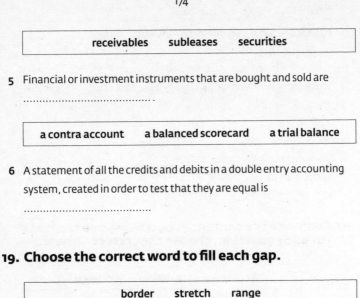

| receivables | subleases | securities |

5 Financial or investment instruments that are bought and sold are

....

| a contra account | a balanced scorecard | a trial balance |

6 A statement of all the credits and debits in a double entry accounting
system, created in order to test that they are equal is

....

19. Choose the correct word to fill each gap.

| border | stretch | range |

1 Prices for her jewelry .... from $40 to $4,500.

| tight | firm | short |

2 Any increase in the cost of materials would be a disaster when our
margins are already so ....

| signs | extends | expires |

3 We will not be renewing our contract with them when this one

....

| take over | take out | make up |

4 We decided to .... a loan to buy some new
equipment.